MONTREAL, 1701

Planting the Tree of Peace

MONTREAL, 1701

Planting the Tree of Peace

GILLES HAVARD

Translated by Phyllis Aronoff
and Howard Scott

Recherches amérindiennes au Québec
McCord Museum of Canadian History
Montreal 2001

MONTREAL, 1701: Planting the Tree of Peace

ISBN 2-920366-29-7

Legal deposit: third quarter 2001

Bibliothèque nationale du Québec

This book is adapted from
*La Grande Paix de Montréal de 1701:
Les voies de la diplomatie franco-amérindienne,*
by Gilles Havard (Recherches amérindiennes
au Québec, Montreal, 1992) and its English translation
*The Great Peace of Montreal of 1701:
French–Native Diplomacy in the Seventeenth Century,*
(McGill-Queen's University Press, Montreal, 2001)

Cover illustration by François Girard
© Vidéanthrop Inc., 2000
Cover design by Épicentre

Book design by Épicentre
Translation by Phyllis Aronoff and Howard Scott
Revision by Judith Turnbull
Proofreading by Jane Jackel

Montreal, 1701 is also available in French.

This publication received a grant from the
ministère de la Culture et des Communications
du Québec and from the Historica Foundation.

Contents

Acknowledgements

This book would not have been possible without the contribution of several people. I wish to express my most sincere thanks to Dominique Legros and Daniel Chevrier of Recherches amérindiennes au Québec and to Moira McCaffrey of the McCord Museum, who encouraged and supported the project. Dominique and Moira's careful reading of the text and pertinent suggestions are deeply appreciated. I also wish to thank Wanda Romer Taylor, Publisher at the McCord, who supervised the preparation, revisions and production of the book. I owe my gratitude as well to Marie-Chantal Anctil, Research Assistant, and Guislaine Lemay, Curatorial Assistant, both at the McCord, who helped with the images and captions, and especially to Marie-Chantal for her meticulous work of checking facts and bibliographic references. My thanks to Phyllis Aronoff and Howard Scott, who translated the original into English; Judith Turnbull, who successfully undertook the huge task of adapting and revising the text; Hélène Joly, who edited the French text; and Jane Jackel, who proofread the final version. I would also like to thank McGill-Queen's University Press for permission to reproduce the maps, and particularly Aurèle Parisien and Susanne McAdam, who worked in close collaboration with Recherches amérindiennes au Québec and the McCord Museum. Finally, my deepest gratitude to Denys Delâge for his comments and constant support, as well as to my sister Calissia for her readings of the text.

GH
JUNE 2001

7

Preface

The Great Peace of Montreal of 1701 was a major event in North American history. Yet few of us — Quebecers, Canadians, or Aboriginal peoples — know of it today.

And yet this was the peace treaty that put an end to almost a century of war between the French and their Native allies on the one hand and the Five Nations Iroquois on the other. Thirty-nine Aboriginal nations sent ambassadors to Montreal from such far-flung areas as Illinois, the Great Lakes region, James Bay, Acadia, Iroquoia and the St. Lawrence "settlements." The conference was a spectacular event, making Montreal the intercultural crossroads of North America.

Ten years ago Gilles Havard, an exceptional young French historian specializing in the history of French-Native relations in New France, opened the door on this little-known period of our past. In these pages, he does so again. Sketching out the broad lines of the period leading up to the signing of the treaty, Havard describes a time when Aboriginal peoples had not been relegated to the historical background, or represented — as they were throughout the 19th and 20th centuries — as mere supporting actors, musket fodder, torturers of missionaries, or, more recently, as passive victims of colonization and assimilation. In this book, the Aboriginal peoples play the part they truly played, as autonomous agents with their own interests, strategies, ceremonies and manners of dress. No longer do they appear under the abstract category of "Indians," but as people and individuals who, like the Huron-Petun chief Kondiaronk or the Potawatomi chief Onanguicé, helped to fashion the country's history.

Havard's work shows clearly that Native peoples did not simply give in to European forms of speech and action. In those times, cultural differences were, to some extent, respected on both sides. Indeed, at the signing of the Great Peace treaty, French officers clad in the courtly attire of France adopted many aspects of Native protocol, such as using wampum belts; participating in condolence ceremonies for the dead; smoking peace pipes; and even dancing in silk stockings and powdered wigs to the beat of Native drums, mirroring the steps and gestures of Hurons, Iroquois, and many other peoples. What a fine feast this was! Surely this event deserves to be firmly engraved in our collective memory.

In addition to restoring Aboriginal faces and identities to history, Gilles Havard is determined to debunk the usual clichés that litter conventional history and our distorted memory of past centuries. He establishes that the Iroquois — contrary to the picture we are usually given — were not always at war with the French. Well before the Great Peace of 1701, there were several attempted alliances between the two peoples. And a considerable number of Iroquois, among them, ancestors of our Mohawk fellow citizens of today, became allies of the French from the 1660s, building their longhouses close to Montreal, and founding the Christianized villages of Kahnawake (Sault St. Louis) and La Montagne. These Iroquois lived and traded with the colonists just as their descendants continue to do today.

Lastly, Havard helps us better grasp the nature of French colonialism, which was founded primarily on an alliance with Native peoples, and thus partly — despite the dynamic of colonization and attempted conversion — on respect for their way of life and their cultures. There could have been no New France, and hence no Canada, without Aboriginal peoples.

As long ago as 1883, the poet Walt Whitman expressed his dismay at his compatriots' indifference to the seeming disappearance of Aboriginal cultures from the continent: "As America develops, adapts, entwines, faithfully identifies its own — are we to see it cheerfully accepting using all the contributions of foreign lands from the whole outside globe — and then rejecting the only ones distinctively its own?"

We might ask the same question today. As Quebec and Canada forge their identities from the wealth of cultures that have been and are still being brought to these shores by immigrants from all corners of the globe, will we welcome and celebrate this enrichment while failing to fully acknowledge the vibrant cultures indigenous to the Americas — the First Nations?

For those of us who are heir to this world of blended cultures, a world both distant and ever-present, this 300th anniversary of the Great Peace of 1701 is an opportunity for reflection. Although there is no question of bringing back the events of this period, they can nevertheless inspire us in our current negotiations, helping us to achieve intercultural agreement, respect and reconciliation between the various First Nations of Canada and mainstream Quebec and Canadian society.

DOMINIQUE LEGROS
President
Recherches amérindiennes au Québec

MOIRA McCAFFREY
Director, Research and Exhibitions
McCord Museum of Canadian History

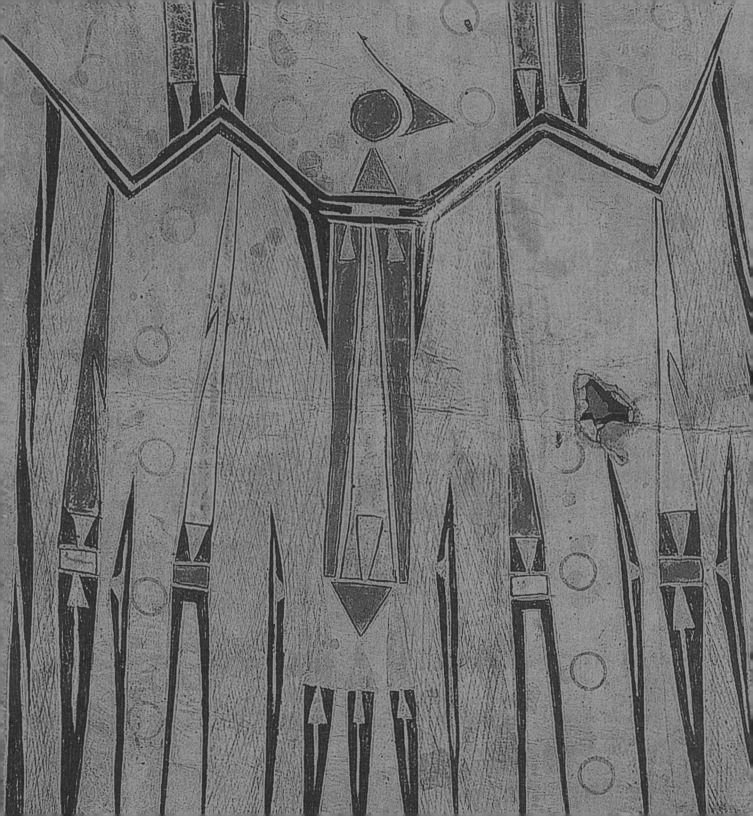

Introduction

In the heat of the summer of 1701, hundreds of Native people paddled their slender birchbark canoes down the Ottawa River, through the vast forests of the Laurentian Basin. Shooting the rapids, avoiding the rocks, they made their way towards Montreal, towards the rising sun. The impressive flotilla was made up of delegations from many nations of the Great Lakes region, known as the *pays d'en haut*. They came from Michilimackinac (Odawas, Huron-Petuns), Green Bay (Potawatomis, Sauks, Menominees, Winnebagos), the area south of Lake Michigan (Mascoutens, Miamis), and the shores of Lake Superior (Crees, Ojibwas). Converging on Montreal from other directions were ambassadors of the Iroquois League, an Abenaki delegation from Acadia, and delegates from the mission villages, or *réductions*, within the French colony. In total, about 1,300 Native delegates, representing 39 nations, would gather in the little colonial town. Their purpose was to participate in a general peace conference — or, to use one of their metaphors, to "bury the hatchet deep in the earth" — in order to put an end to decades of warfare between the Five Nations Iroquois on one side and the French and their Native allies on the other.

Founded in 1642, Montreal had developed substantially as a result of the expansion of the fur trade into the *pays d'en haut* and the subsequent broadening, from the 1660s on, of the French-Native alliance. As the gateway to a hinterland abounding in furs, Montreal was a vital centre of diplomacy and trade. From June to September, the town received Native ambassadors from the west and sometimes from Iroquoia. It was in a sense the summer capital of Canada.

The events of 1701 marked a dramatic development in New World politics. That year King Louis XIV of France (the "Sun King") inaugurated a new imperial policy for North America, decreeing that New France, including the colony of Louisiana, should henceforth attempt to block English expansion into the interior of the continent. Among the actions to serve this end was the convening of a general peace conference in Montreal in August 1701. The treaty that resulted — known as the Great Peace of Montreal — finally ended the Iroquois Wars, ostensibly bringing peace to the vast territory extending from Acadia in the east to the Mississippi in the west, and from James Bay in the north to Missouri in the south.

Part One

17TH-CENTURY WAR AND PEACE

The French-Native Alliance and the Five Nations Iroquois

Alliances with Native peoples were crucial to the survival of New France. The first such alliance was formed at the beginning of the 17th century, in the time of the French explorer Samuel de Champlain. French fur traders in the St. Lawrence region established ties first with the Montagnais and then with the Algonquins, thus connecting their trade to a network that extended as far as the Great Lakes and Hudson Bay and included the powerful Hurons, the Nipissings, the Neutrals, and the Petuns. Within a few years, the Hurons and the French had sealed a lasting alliance. In exchange for European goods (copper pots, knives, hatchets, cloth, guns), the French obtained pelts, in particular, highly desirable beaver pelts. In accordance with the rules of Native diplomacy, this trade was based on trust and loyalty, and the partners had to demonstrate mutual generosity by exchanging gifts and people (through "adoption") and assisting each other militarily. Champlain was obliged several times (in 1609, 1610, and 1615) to join his Huron, Algonquin, and Montagnais allies in military expeditions against the Iroquois.

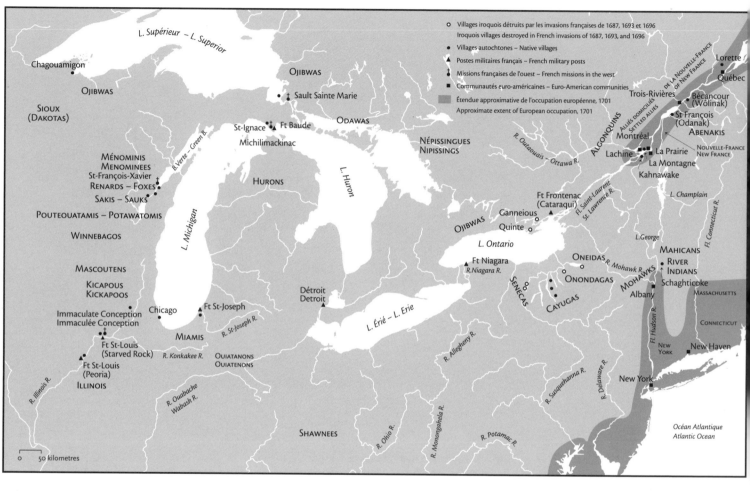

Native and Euro-American Settlements, around 1701. Adapted with permission from *The Great Peace of Montreal of 1701: French–Native Diplomacy in the Seventeenth Century.* McGill-Queen's University Press, Montreal, 2001

THE IROQUOIS: PEOPLE OF THE LONGHOUSE

The Iroquois (the name given by the French to the Haudenosaunees, "the people of the longhouse") were well established in the area south and east of Lake Ontario early in the 17th century, with a population of 20,000 to 30,000. They were a semi-sedentary people whose food supply was based on corn. Their palisaded villages contained between 30 and 150 longhouses, large structures (sometimes as long as 60 metres) that could house many families. Iroquois society was organized matrilineally (that is, it was based on the female line). Like the Hurons, Petuns, Eries, and Neutrals, the Iroquois belonged to the Iroquoian-language family. In the 17th century, five Iroquois nations were united within a confederacy. The Iroquois League, according to oral tradition, was founded by the heroic figure Deganawidah, who urged his people to put an end to past quarrels and establish an Iroquois "Great Peace." The confederacy comprised the Mohawks, the "keepers of the eastern door" of the longhouse; the Oneidas; the Onondagas, the "keepers of the fire" and the holders of the wampum belts; the Cayugas; and the Senecas, the "keepers of the western door." In 1722 the Tuscaroras joined the League to make it the Six Nations. The chiefs, chosen from the village clans, represented each nation at the League council in Onondaga, the Iroquois capital. Traditionally, the council was made up of 50 hereditary members.

After 1615, the French avoided participating in these raids. In fact, in the 1630s Champlain hoped to establish trade and diplomatic ties with the four western nations of the Iroquois League. But it was with the fifth Iroquois nation, the Mohawks, that Governor Montmagny signed a peace treaty in 1645, one that also included his converted allies. This peace was broken the following year, and the Five Nations gradually increased their attacks, warring with several nations. The Iroquois had the advantage of their geographic position, which enabled them to get material support — particularly firearms — from their Dutch allies. Unlike the Dutch, the French did not sell guns to their allies, except to those who had been baptized.

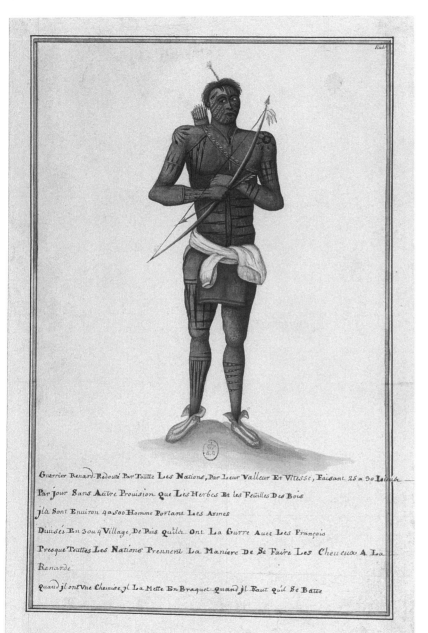

Guerrier Renard. Redouté Par Toutte Les Nations, Par Leur Valleur Et Vitesse, Faisant 25 a 30 Lieüe

Par Jour Sans Autre Prouision Que Les Herbes Et les Feüilles Des Bois

jla Sont Enuiron 4 a 500 Homme Portant Les Armes

Diuisés En 3 ou 4 Village, De Puis qu'ila Ont La Gurre Auec Les François

Presque Toutles Les Nations Prennent La Maniere De Se Faire Les Cheueux A La

Renarde

Quand jl ont Vne Chemise jl La Mette En Braquet Quand jl Faut Qu'il Se Batte

WARS OF CAPTURE

Native wars in the 17th century, though often interpreted as economic conflicts, were in fact wars of capture. For example, Iroquois warfare allowed for the capture and assimilation of prisoners. War parties were usually formed on the initiative of a grief-stricken clan mother, who would present a wampum belt to some young warriors and urge them to bring her back prisoners or, failing that, scalps "to appease the soul of her husband, her son, or her close relation," as the Jesuit father Charlevoix explained. Most prisoners were in fact adopted and then integrated into lineages in such great numbers that in the 1660s two-thirds of the Iroquois League consisted of prisoners. Warriors of the Five Nations also captured increasing numbers of enemies to counteract the fall in population caused by epidemics of European origin.

Fox Warrior, about 1710. Watercolour, artist unknown. Bibliothèque nationale de France, Paris

Although attempts were made in the 1650s to forge an alliance between the French and the four western Iroquois nations, hostilities intensified to the point where, around 1660, the future of the colony was jeopardized. In 1665 the Carignan-Salières Regiment, 1,200 strong, landed at the town of Quebec with the intention of invading Iroquoia. The regiment's expeditions did not inflict heavy losses on the enemy, but they were damaging enough to persuade the Iroquois, in 1667, to negotiate a general peace with the representatives of the Sun King and his Native allies.

The peace settlement opened up the *pays d'en haut* to the French, and soon hundreds of *coureurs des bois*, missionaries, and soldiers made their way to the region. Peace also allowed the mending of the colony's network of alliances, which had been destabilized by the destruction of Huronia around 1650. This network, which included dozens of nations, was formed around five principal partners: the Odawas, the Hurons (at least those who had taken refuge in the Great Lakes region and had been joined by the Petuns), the Potawatomis, the Ojibwas, and the French. The French were also allied with the members of the Abenaki (Wabanaki) Confederacy (Pentagouets, Passamaquoddys, Maliseets, Mi'kmaqs), the Algonquins, the Montagnais, and the Native peoples in the colony's mission villages (including the Iroquois of Montreal).

NATIVE PEOPLES OF THE MISSION VILLAGES

In the second half of the 17th century, Native villages were established within the French colony on the St. Lawrence. The French called the inhabitants *domiciliés*, because they were permanently settled there. These communities consisted mostly of Christian converts originally from Georgian Bay (Hurons), New England (Abenakis), or Iroquoia. The Hurons settled in the Quebec region in 1650 after the destruction of their confederation by the Iroquois. They established a permanent settlement at Wendake (Lorette) in 1697. Some Abenakis, fleeing English colonists, sought refuge with the French in the late 1670s, establishing two villages on the St. Lawrence, Odanak (St. François) and Wolinak (Bécancour). Iroquois converts — mostly Mohawks and Oneidas — began migrating to Montreal in 1667 and formed two communities: Kahnawake (Sault St. Louis), two leagues south of Montreal; and La Montagne, a Sulpician mission located at what is now the intersection of Atwater and Sherbrooke Streets in Montreal. La Montagne also included Hurons, Nipissings, and Algonquins. The inhabitants of these villages remained autonomous. They fought alongside their French allies, teaching them the art of war in the woods. In the 1680s, the Montreal Iroquois played a key role in the defence of the colony.

Jacques-René de Brisay, Marquis de Denonville, before 1710. Artist unknown. David Ross McCord Collection, McCord Museum, Montreal, M1831

The French-Iroquois conflict flared up again in the 1680s. In retaliation for Iroquois attacks against allies in the *pays d'en haut* and to safeguard New France's economic interests, Governor La Barre, in 1684, and his successor, Denonville, in 1687, sent French-Native expeditions against the Senecas. The first failed miserably, but the second ended with the destruction of four Iroquois villages, abandoned by their inhabitants. In subsequent years, conflict spread to the colony itself in the context of the War of the League of Augsburg (1688–1697), which pitted France against England and other countries. The Iroquois attack on Lachine in 1689 marked the beginning of this round of hostilities. Frontenac, Denonville's successor as governor, attempted to re-establish diplomatic dialogue, but then he too adopted a policy of force, attacking the Mohawks in 1693 and the Onondagas and Oneidas in 1696 and encouraging his western allies to harass the Iroquois.

Peace Strategies

THE FRENCH

For the French, the conflict with the Iroquois was an obstacle to the development of the colony. Governors Frontenac (1689–1698) and Callière (1698–1703) ardently desired peace, but they wanted to dictate the terms. First of all, they wanted to negotiate a treaty with the whole of the Iroquois League, and to do so independently of the English. They also wanted a "general" peace agreement, one that would include their allies in the *pays d'en haut.* To accomplish this, they had to reaffirm the French-Native alliance and short-circuit any attempt by the Iroquois and the Great Lakes nations to make a separate peace.

LOUIS HECTOR DE CALLIÈRE

Louis Hector de Callière had taken part in several of Louis XIV's campaigns when he was appointed governor of Montreal in 1684, at the age of 36. A stern, sometimes authoritarian man, Callière served as a devoted and competent officer for some 20 years in New France, at ease both in military affairs and politics. Quickly gaining expertise in guerrilla warfare, he fortified Montreal and its surroundings to ward off enemy attacks and took part in expeditions into the heart of Iroquoia, assisting Denonville in 1687 and Frontenac in 1696. Callière proved himself a shrewd diplomat in his many meetings with Iroquois ambassadors and a clear-sighted strategist with respect to the geopolitical situation of New France, qualities that prepared him well for the negotiations of 1700-1701. When Frontenac died in 1698, Callière became governor general of the colony. He was officially appointed to the position in the spring of 1699 following a request by his brother François, secretary of the king's cabinet. Callière died in Quebec in May 1703, "much regretted," according to Charlevoix, "as the most accomplished general this colony has ever had."

There was a double paradox in the French policy. In order to bring the Iroquois to the peace table, France had to get them in a stranglehold, and the most effective way to achieve that was to encourage its allies to fight them — hardly the conditions for a general peace. Furthermore, a peace that included the Iroquois and the nations of the west, though desirable, might eventually weaken the French position. Since the time of Champlain, the Iroquois had served as a barrier between New France's Native allies and the English or Dutch merchants. The French did not want to destroy the Iroquois, only to weaken them.

THE IROQUOIS

The Five Nations Iroquois were indeed weakened. In 1694 the Onondaga chief Sadekarnaktie lamented to representatives of New York: "The grease is melted from our flesh and drops on our neighbours, who are grown fat and live at ease while we become lean. They flourish and we decrease." From 1689 to 1698, the number of Iroquois warriors fell from 2,550 to 1,230. This decline can be attributed to epidemics and the emigration of Mohawks and Oneidas to the mission villages near Montreal, but also to war. French expeditions had severely damaged Iroquois cornfields, and warriors from the Great Lakes had frequently returned to their villages with Iroquois scalps. The Iroquois recognized that they needed the French to arrange a truce with the nations of the west. A general peace agreement could bring the nations allied with the French into the Covenant Chain; it could make it easier for the Iroquois to hunt in the Great Lakes region; and it could counter internal factionalism by establishing Iroquois neutrality with respect to the rival empires of the French and the English.

THE COVENANT CHAIN

Two cross-cultural networks of alliances were formed during the first half of the 17th century, that of the French, the Hurons, and their allies, and that of the Iroquois and the Dutch (and later the English). The latter was known as the Covenant Chain. The "chain" had its origins in the treaty that the Dutch colonists negotiated with the Mahicans (neighbours of the Mohawks) in 1618. This agreement was symbolized by a rope mooring a Dutch ship to a tree planted in Native territory. The Mohawks changed the rope into a steel chain with the alliance treaty that they negotiated in 1643. The English of New York, who replaced the Dutch in 1664, renewed the chain, including all of the Five Nations Iroquois. In 1677 the chain became silver through two peace treaties negotiated in Albany. These treaties inaugurated the Covenant Chain as a multilateral alliance of English colonies with several Native nations under the supervision of the Iroquois.

The Iroquois of the League and the Iroquois in the mission villages had concluded their own peace agreement in 1696. This rapprochement, which deprived the French colony of the military cooperation of its allies in Kahnawake and La Montagne, contributed greatly to the peace process that led to the treaty of 1701. The Christian Iroquois, who had always maintained political links with the League, would play an active diplomatic role in support of the talks. As allies of both the French and the League, they could readily act as intermediaries.

THE NATIONS OF THE *PAYS D'EN HAUT*

The Great Lakes nations were divided among those in favour of war, those in favour of a separate peace with the Iroquois, and those in favour of a general peace under the auspices of the French governor. The latter option was preferred by influential chiefs such as the Huron Kondiaronk, who wanted to recover prisoners taken by the Iroquois, prevent a separate French-Iroquois peace, and reinforce the alliance with the French. Some of those who favoured a general peace probably also wanted to gain greater access to the Albany (English) market and thereby be able to preserve their independence by playing on intercolonial competition.

Delicate Negotiations, 1697–1701

FIRST STEPS, 1697–1699

In 1697 there began a period of intense diplomatic activity that would lead, four years later, to the Great Peace of Montreal. Talks between the French and the Iroquois, broken off in 1695, were resumed a few months after Governor Frontenac's military expedition against the Oneidas and Onondagas. In November 1697 in Quebec, the Onondaga sachem (chief) Aradgi, speaking for the four western Iroquois nations, expressed the desire to build a solid peace with the French and to forget the "nasty business of the past." But at that time there was no consensus within the League.

THE IROQUOIS FACTIONS

The political organization of Native peoples in northeastern North America was based neither on coercive power (the chiefs did not impose anything, they proposed) nor on majority rule, but on the rule of consensus. It was thus often hard to establish a unified position. The Iroquois League, in particular, had enormous difficulty reconciling its factions. There were not only divisions among the nations, but also tensions within villages and clans. The virulence of Iroquois factionalism in the late 17th century is explained by pressure from the colonies and by the diversity of the population, due to the absorption of prisoners of war. At the very end of the century, there were three factions in Iroquois political life. The "pro-French" faction was determined to accept French conditions for peace even if that meant breaking the chain that bound them to New York. At the other extreme was the "pro-English" faction, which rejected the idea of any agreement with the French, preferring to maintain an exclusive alliance with the English. In the middle were the proponents of neutrality, who wanted to guarantee the political independence of the Iroquois League through a strategy of balance between the two competing empires. The Onondaga chief Teganissorens embodied this third option, believing that it offered the best chance of preserving the League's unity.

In January 1698 Montreal received word that the Treaty of Ryswick had been signed in Europe the preceding autumn, ending the War of the League of Augsburg. The Iroquois could no longer use the English military threat to New France to their own advantage. With peace established between the British and French crowns, New York encouraged the Iroquois, whom they claimed as their subjects, to make peace with New France, but to do so under New York's auspices. The French, on the other hand, wanted to make a separate peace with the Iroquois.

In March 1699 three Iroquois sachems — two Onondagas and one Oneida — arrived in Montreal with three French prisoners and spoke to Governor Callière on behalf of the Five Nations. They asked him to stop the raids by the Great Lakes nations and called for an exchange of prisoners in Albany, "where the great business of peace will be concluded." Callière answered that there would be no peace concluded except in Montreal, that French officers would then be dispatched to Iroquoia to recover the "young Frenchmen and allied [Native people]" held prisoner, and that peace could be negotiated only "jointly with all the allies." The governor granted them a 60-day truce, but he was speaking only for his allies in the mission villages and the Algonquins, not for the nations of the west. In mid-September, while sachems from the four western Iroquois nations were meeting with the English in Albany, seeking help in stopping the raids, a delegation of Onondagas met with Callière in Quebec, asking for an exchange of prisoners. They also pleaded for a stop to the raids. "I beseech you, my father," an Iroquois orator had said to the French governor, "make your allies stop coming into our territory every day to split our heads." Callière refused both requests.

ONONTIO AND HIS "CHILDREN"

The name "Onontio" ("Great Mountain") is the literal translation into Huron-Iroquois of the name of the first governor of New France, Montmagny (1638–1648). It was used from 1640 on by the Hurons and picked up a little later by the Iroquois. Until 1760 this was the term most often used by the Native people for all the governors general of New France. When they did not call the governor Onontio, they referred to him as their father. This practice was probably started by the French, but it fit in with the Native diplomatic tradition, since Aboriginal people customarily used the language of kinship (grandfather, uncle, father, cousin, son, nephew, etc.) to designate an ally. For Native peoples, the image of the father did not imply subordination or coercion. They saw the power of the governor as being like that of their chiefs. His orders were interpreted not as inflexible commands, but as proposals to be debated; and his authority extended no further than his generosity.

The Decisive Year, 1700

The Iroquois resolved in 1700 to resume talks with New France and the Great Lakes nations, and thus to follow a course of action independent of New York. They arranged a truce with some groups in the west, giving them access to the Albany market, but failed to form an alliance with all of them. After a consensus was reached on the French demands, an Iroquois delegation met with the French in Montreal in July. The Iroquois orator Tonatakout promised to undertake a general exchange of French captives and Native prisoners from the western nations, "so that none would remain." He asked Callière to send three Frenchmen — Father Bruyas, Chabert de Joncaire, and Le Moyne de Maricourt — to return with the delegation to Iroquoia to oversee the exchange. The governor agreed and proposed that they meet again later in the summer in Montreal.

The Iroquois ambassadors had chosen well when they selected Father Bruyas, Joncaire, and Maricourt as representatives of the French; these three were well respected by the Iroquois. Joncaire had been adopted by the Senecas, Maricourt by the Onondagas, and Father Bruyas had served as a missionary to the Oneidas and the Mohawks. In welcoming them to Iroquoia, an elder declared, "Now we no longer doubt the uprightness and sincerity in the heart of our father, Onontio, who sent us the Black Robe [Bruyas] and our son Joncaire. Our land will become beautiful. You will be witnesses to the faith of all our warriors when you enter our village."

The Five Nations were clearly moving towards a neutral course of action. Speaking for the League council, the Onondaga sachem Teganissorens addressed a British representative named Van Eps in the presence of Bruyas and Maricourt: "You will say to my brother Corlard [the governor of New York] that I will go down to Montreal where my father, Onontio, has lighted the fire of peace. I will also go to Orange [Albany]: my brother calls me, and so that there is nothing you do not know, here is the wampum belt that I will carry to my father Onontio."

WAMPUM

Wampum collars or belts, as the contemporary author Lahontan wrote, were "a kind of contract without which it is impossible to conclude any significant business with the [Native people]." The French therefore had dozens of them made by Native women in 1701. The belts consisted of cylindrical beads crafted from polished and drilled marine shell and threaded in rows to form rectangular bands or sometimes single strings. Their size, their colour, and the symbols created by the alternation of white and purple (often called black) beads were never random. A belt had great symbolic value in negotiations; the colour white signified peace and life, purple symbolized mourning, and a belt painted red meant war. The purpose of wampum was to validate, in a ritualized way, the words that were spoken. After reciting the proposal that accompanied each belt, the speaker laid the wampum at the feet of the person addressed. Its acceptance meant that the message would be taken into consideration, but it could also be rejected. It was not the wampum itself that was important to Native people, but its use and the process of gift exchange that resulted from its acceptance. In the absence of wampum, one could use animal pelts, tobacco, axes, clothing, or even prisoners. Because of the symbols woven into wampum, however, it had an archival value, serving to preserve the nation's oral memory.

At the end of August 1700, 50 Iroquois sachems went to Albany and 19 others headed for Montreal. In Montreal, a French-Iroquois peace treaty was signed at the conference that took place from 3 to 9 September. The Iroquois from the mission villages of La Montagne and Kahnawake, the Abenakis, the Huron-Petuns (represented by Kondiaronk), and the Odawas also took part in the discussions. Kondiaronk declared: "Onontio ... takes the hatchets of all the nations. For myself, I throw mine at his feet. Who would be bold enough to go against his will, he who is our father here? I do not at all doubt that the people of the *pays d'en haut* will follow what he wishes. It is up to you the Iroquois nations to do so too."

Wampum belt, 18th century. Huron-Wendat, maker unknown. Gift of Mrs. Walter M. Stewart, McCord Museum, Montreal, M20401

KONDIARONK, THE ARCHITECT OF THE PEACE

The Huron-Petun chief Kondiaronk, also called "Le Rat" ("The Muskrat"), was a charismatic figure in the French-Native alliance. Described by La Potherie as "the most able and most eminent person in the nations of the *pays d'en haut*," he embodied all the qualities that were demanded in a chief: generosity, skill in combat, political intelligence, and unequalled eloquence. "Nobody could ever have more wit than he," wrote Father Charlevoix. "He shone ... in private conversations, and people often took pleasure in teasing him just to hear his repartee, which was always lively and colourful, and usually impossible to answer. He was in that the only man in Canada who could match Count Frontenac, who often invited him to his table for the pleasure of his officers."

Kondiaronk was born on the shores of Georgian Bay around 1649, the time of the fall of Huronia. From the early 1680s, he distinguished himself as one of the main chiefs of the Huron-Petun village of Michilimackinac. Unsurpassed as a strategist, Kondiaronk feared more than anything a separate peace between the French and the Iroquois, and he resorted to trickery to break up negotiations between New France's governor Denonville and the Onondaga chief Teganissorens. Kondiaronk later joined the pro-French faction, becoming its leader around 1694–1695, while his rival, Le Baron, led the pro-Iroquois faction. In 1697, leading 150 warriors, he defeated a party of 60 Iroquois in a fierce canoe battle on Lake Erie. "Le Rat was then sincerely attached to the interests of the French," observed Charlevoix. "It was he alone who had prevented all the Hurons of Michilimackinac from following Le Baron to New York." However, Kondiaronk hoped to build a general peace, which could only benefit the Hurons (through a consolidation of the French alliance and a relaxation of tension in relations with the Iroquois and the English).

After the treaty signing of September 1700, Kondiaronk returned to Michilimackinac and told "all the nations of the Lakes" of the events in Montreal, urging them to go there the following August with their Iroquois prisoners. As Charlevoix confirmed unequivocally, Kondiaronk played a pivotal role in building the peace of 1701: "The governor general placed in [Kondiaronk] his main hope for the success of his great enterprise."

A Peace Mission to the Great Lakes, October 1700–June 1701

The peace was fragile — and incomplete. Governor Callière and the chiefs of the Great Lakes nations present at the Montreal conference wanted the peace treaty to include all the nations of the French-Native alliance. Callière dispatched two ambassadors, Le Gardeur de Courtemanche, a soldier and diplomat, and the Jesuit father Jean Enjalran, to the west. Their mission was threefold: first, to inform all the nations of the *pays d'en haut* of the September agreements and have them accept and sign them; second, to convince the allied chiefs to attend a general peace conference in Montreal in August 1701, bringing with them all their Iroquois prisoners; and third, to attempt to put a stop to the war being waged by the Odawas, Miamis, and others against the Sioux. While Father Enjalran spent the winter in Michilimackinac, Courtemanche travelled around Lake Michigan visiting the encampments of many nations. Most of them were still at war with the Iroquois, but most agreed to send delegates to Montreal. Others would overcome their reluctance at a conference at Michilimackinac in May 1701.

The Influence of Chief Teganissorens, May–June 1701

The Onondaga chief Teganissorens came to Montreal in May 1701 with some other sachems to prepare for the August conference. He asked Callière to make reparation for the Odawas' attack against the Iroquois the preceding fall and refused to allow the French to establish a post at Detroit as they were planning. Shortly after this meeting, Callière delegated Bruyas, Joncaire, and Maricourt, and a score of other Frenchmen to conclude the preliminary talks. The English also sent a few ambassadors to the Iroquois capital, to obstruct the French plans and invite the Five Nations to a conference planned in Albany. Teganissorens stated that some delegates should go to Montreal and others to Albany, and that he would remain in Onondaga to symbolize Iroquois neutrality. The "Tree of Peace" had become visible on the horizon.

"THE TREE OF PEACE":
THE USE OF METAPHOR IN THE PEACE NEGOTIATIONS

At the September 1700 peace conference in Montreal, the Huron-Petun chief Kondiaronk said, "The sun today dissipated the clouds to reveal this beautiful Tree of Peace, which was already planted on the highest mountain of the Earth." He was using the language common to Native diplomats, one laced with images, whether the subject was war ("boil the kettle," "toss the hatchet to the sky," "stir the earth"), reconciliation ("weep for the dead," "wrap the bones," "cover the dead"), or peace ("hang up the hatchet," "tie the sun," "plant the Tree of Peace"). Orators at the 1701 peace negotiations used the Iroquois metaphor of the Tree of Peace, a tree to be "planted" or "raised" on "the highest mountain of the Earth" and provided with "deep roots so that it [could] never be uprooted." Its branches and foliage rose "to the heavens," providing "dense shade," so that "those who [sat] under it [were] ... refreshed ... sheltered from any storms that might threaten them," and able to "do good business." The hatchet was another favourite image ("The hatchet is stopped, we have buried it during these days here in the deepest place in the earth, so that it will not be taken up again by one side or the other," etc.). The "kettle" and "big dish" were frequently used to convey an agreement to share hunting territory and not to kill one another when they met ("Let us eat from the same kettle when we meet during the hunt"; they would share the same "dish" as "brothers"; "When we meet, we will look on each other as brothers, we will eat the same meal together").

Sauva

Sauvages atendant
a la porte du Village, celuy
qui porte le Calumet

Villages des Sauvages

Sauvages qui demandent passage

Part Two

> "THE TREE OF PEACE IS PLANTED ON THE HIGHEST MOUNTAIN"

For more than two weeks in the summer of 1701, from 23 July to 7 August, Montreal moved to the rhythm of Aboriginal cultures. The arrival of 1,300 Native delegates brought a remarkable diversity of peoples to the island of Montreal, then inhabited by about 2,600 colonists (of which 1,200 lived in the town itself) and 1,000 settled Native people. An astonishing variety of dress, language, movement, and ceremony made Montreal the stage for a spectacular New World theatre.

The Arrival of the Ambassadors

When the flotillas of delegates from Iroquoia and the Great Lakes arrived in the colony, they did not go directly to Montreal, but stopped for a day in the Iroquois village of Kahnawake. The Onondagas, Cayugas, and Oneidas were the first to arrive, on 21 July. "As soon as they were close enough to see the Fort," wrote Bacqueville de La Potherie, "they saluted it with gun fire," and their brothers from the village, lined up on the bank, responded in the same way.

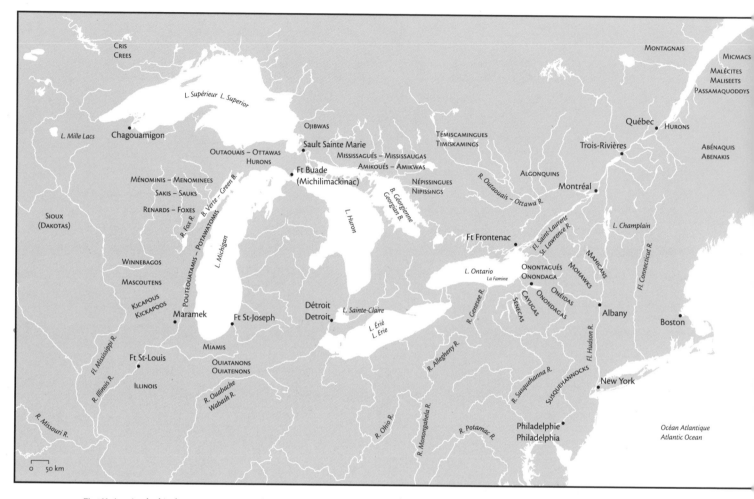

First Nations involved in the peace process, around 1701. Adapted with permission from *The Great Peace of Montreal of 1701: French–Native Diplomacy in the Seventeenth Century*. McGill-Queen's University Press, Montreal, 2001

A council was held shortly afterwards, and a "little fire of dried brambles" was symbolically lit to prepare the Iroquois ambassadors for the great fire that would blaze in Montreal. The guests then smoked "with great composure for a good quarter of an hour," and their hosts addressed them with customary eloquence. "My brothers," the chief of Kahnawake said, "we are happy to see you here having escaped all the perils along the way. Indeed, how many accidents could have befallen you? How many rocks or rapids where you could have perished if you did not have all the skill ... that you have always shown in perilous circumstances?" Carrying three strings of wampum, the chief then performed the condolence ceremony — the wiping of tears, the clearing of the ears, and the opening of the throat — to prepare them for the coming peace talks.

The next day, just when the Iroquois were leaving for Montreal, the flotillas from the Great Lakes arrived. "All the delegates and important persons" from the *pays d'en haut* were ushered into the longhouse of an Iroquois chief. There they performed their distinctive calumet (peace pipe) dance while the welcoming feast was prepared in a neighbouring hut. An Odawa delegate entertained the crowd by skilfully manipulating a red stone pipe decorated with feathers, and 12 men in a circle sang to the rhythm of their rattles. "There was a chief who stood up a quarter of an hour later," reported La Potherie, "and, taking a hatchet, struck a post with it. The musicians immediately fell silent. 'I killed,' he said, 'four

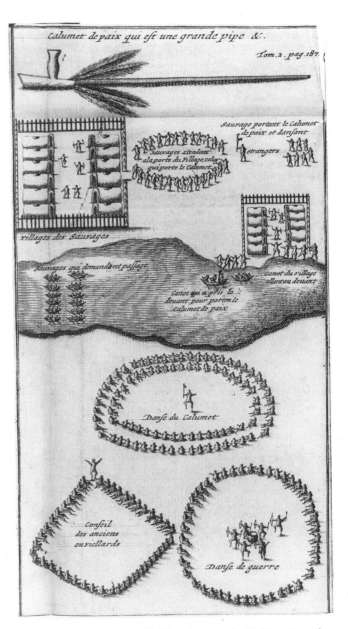

Detail taken from *Nouveaux voyages de Mr. Le baron de Lahontan, dans l'Amérique septentrionale …* Louis Armand de Lom d'Arce, Baron de Lahontan. Chez les Frères l'Honoré, La Haye, 1703

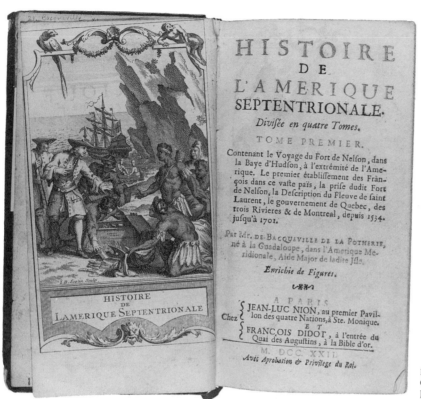

Frontispiece of *Histoire de l'Amérique septentrionale…*
Claude-Charles Le Roy Bacqueville de la Potherie,
Jean-Luc Nion et François Didot, Paris, 1722

BACQUEVILLE DE LA POTHERIE, WITNESS TO THE GREAT PEACE

It is thanks to Bacqueville de La Potherie that we know the details of the Montreal conference. Born in Paris in 1663, La Potherie was in 1698 appointed comptroller of the marine and of the fortifications in New France. His *Histoire de l'Amérique Septentrionale,* published in 1722, is an invaluable work on the history of New France. La Potherie, to his regret, played no official role in the negotiations leading up to the Great Peace of Montreal, but he took an intense interest in them. He was present in Kahnawake on 21 and 22 July 1701 and then in Montreal during the following weeks. La Potherie was an attentive observer who meticulously recorded Native protocol observed during the ceremonies of the Great Peace of Montreal.

Iroquois five years ago' ... and, tearing off a piece of tobacco, 'I take this as a medicine to restore my spirit.' The Musicians applauded him with shouts and rapid movements of their gourds, the sound of two to three hundred [Native people] was heard from one end of the hut to the other." The ritual of the calumet and of the speeches, to the beat of dances and songs, served to dissipate tensions between hosts and visitors, and foster feelings of understanding, friendship, and peace.

The next day, the ambassadors from the west entered Montreal. When they came within "musket range of the town," the 200 canoes formed a single line. The canoeists fired their guns and uttered "great cries" and the French responded with a cannon salute. After landing and storing their canoes, the delegates built birchbark huts along the palisades, between the town and the river. "Care was taken," noted La Potherie, "to have brought to them quantities of tree branches to shelter them from the sun." The Iroquois of the League received even more attention; some were accommodated in the residence of Le Moyne Maricourt. Having been adopted by the Iroquois, Maricourt was quite comfortable playing host to them.

The Senecas reached Montreal that same day. The French diplomat Joncaire welcomed their "great chief" Tekanoet, 80 years old, who stood in his canoe and lamented the dead according to custom. Joncaire took the old sachem by the arm and, in accordance with the condolence ceremony, led him, hand in hand with the other chiefs, to the location for the grand council, where Governor Callière awaited. In the afternoon, Callière assembled all the allied chiefs in his courtyard. Some sat on chairs, others on the ground, and the Huron chief Kondiaronk gave the first speech, "in the name of the allied nations."

The Montreal Trade Fair

Parallel to the peace talks was the business of trading furs. The trading officially began on 25 July at an assembly attended by Callière and the Odawas, after which the Native delegates gave gifts to the French governor. The town gates were opened, and the Native traders could enter the town freely with their furs, to visit the shops of the French merchants. "They were sold powder, shot, hats, clothing in the French style trimmed with fake gold lace ... vermilion, kettles, iron and copper pots, and all sorts of hardware," wrote La Potherie.

The Montreal trade fair, which had existed since the 1660s, was traditionally an occasion of great excitement. Disturbances were not uncommon, and this year the colonial authorities had to be especially cautious, given the unusual presence of 1,300 visitors, not to mention the political significance of the conference. To prevent trouble, the governor and the intendant issued an order prohibiting the sale of alcohol during the conference. Many Native chiefs expressed their approval. "What made it so easy to execute this order," reported Intendant Beauharnois the following year, "was that the public had an interest in complying, in order to contribute to the conclusion of a general peace treaty so necessary to the colony ... devastated by the long, cruel war."

Trade issues were the focus of serious debate at the conference, betraying persistent problems in the French-Native alliance. Outoutagan, speaking for the four Odawa nations, told Callière at a special council meeting: "We have destroyed and eaten all the land. There are few beavers now, and we can only hunt bear, wild cats, and various small pelts." The Potawatomi chief Onanguicé exhorted Callière "to have pity on them, and give them good prices on merchandise, because they had few beaver pelts." While clearly these chiefs were warning the French that the numbers of beaver were in decline, their words were also metaphorical and symbolic in nature. The chiefs wanted to elicit compassion from the French and encourage them to be generous in trade.

Two styles of trade were in conflict: on the European side, the concept of profit and the law of supply and demand; and on the Aboriginal side, gift giving, reciprocity, and general trade, regardless of the availability of goods. The French merchants did not go along with the logic of reciprocity, as Outoutagan was quite aware. "It is useless to ask you for low prices [for European goods]," he told Callière, "because we know very well that each one is master of his goods. At least ask them [the merchants] ... that they be at the same price as last year." The Amikwas drew attention to "the consideration they had shown in not trading ... with the English, who sold to them at better prices." Since the Great Lakes allies believed that the French were not being generous enough, they refused to relinquish the option of trading in Albany. Callière therefore felt obliged, for political reasons, to accept the role of provider. He had gifts distributed to the delegates at each discussion — bread, a small quantity of wine, blankets, gunpowder, and so forth. He also promised to urge the merchants to adjust their prices.

The administrative and merchant elites of the colony knew that they had to take care not to exploit Native traders. As an anonymous chronicler stated in 1705, "A certain balance must be maintained in the setting of prices, both with respect to the [Native people], who must not be discouraged by a low estimate of the value of their beaver, and with respect to the price the English pay." A compromise was thus developed in the style of trade in Montreal. While the French merchants could continue to make a profit, they had to take into account the socio-political conditions of the French-Native alliance and the desire of the Native people to have the governor provide for them.

The Epidemic

Despite the excitement of commerce and the optimism of the peace talks, a pall lay over the conference. A "violent cold" had overcome many delegates. They were victims of an epidemic like those that had drastically reduced the Native population of northeastern North America in the 17th century. In the spring of 1701, rumours of an epidemic in Montreal had reached the *pays d'en haut,* and events would prove them well founded. Some delegates died from sickness on the way to Montreal, and some turned back, afraid to continue the journey. "Out of one fleet of 180 canoes ... 30 were forced to put in to shore because of illness," explained the Jesuit priest, Father Charlevoix. This was the case for the Illinois. The persistence of those who carried on was proof of their extraordinary determination to pursue the general peace.

THE NON-PARTICIPANTS

Certain Native groups did not take part in the negotiations for the Great Peace of Montreal. The absence of the Montagnais is not very surprising. Though traditional allies of the French, they had been only peripherally affected by the Iroquois Wars of the second half of the 17th century and had not taken part in the subsequent peace negotiations. The absence of the Hurons of Lorette is more surprising. They had joined the French in military expeditions in Iroquoia and had been represented at the conference with Iroquois League ambassadors held in Montreal in July 1700. It is possible that they were represented by other groups in 1701; however, this remains uncertain. The case of the Dakota Sioux is different; the French had wanted to include them in the general peace but Native allies of the French refused.

In his address on 23 July, Kondiaronk referred to the epidemic: "Our father, you see us near your mat; it is not without having endured many dangers on such a long voyage. The falls, the rapids, and a thousand other obstacles did not seem so difficult for us to surmount because of the desire we had to see you and to gather together here. We found many of our brothers dead along the river [because of] sickness ... However, we made a bridge of all those bodies, on which we walked with determination ... You must judge from that how much we have been tested."

Many chiefs were so ill that they had difficulty speaking before Callière, and some died. The epidemic must have led Callière to rush the discussions, and it created tension between the French and their allies. The Native people had long been aware that the epidemics originated with the Europeans. They thought of the newcomers, especially the priests, as sorcerers, all the more powerful because their own shamans were helpless before the new diseases. During the conference, it was even rumoured that "the French had gathered so many peoples in their territory only in order to destroy them."

The Return of Prisoners: A Stumbling Block in the Peace Process

Every day from 25 July to 1 August, the governor received the Native ambassadors with great ceremony. On 2 and 3 August, the private sessions were replaced by public meetings with either the Great Lakes nations or the Iroquois. While all the various participants of the Montreal conference sought to make peace, an important problem nearly undermined the entire agreement.

Prisoner exchange had for many years been a thorny issue in negotiations with Native nations. This procedure, commonplace for Europeans, could not easily be adapted to Native societies. In these societies, captives, whether European or Native, were usually put to death or adopted by families to replace their dead. Releasing a prisoner was like losing a relative. Even so, the general peace was viewed by many of the Native nations as an opportunity (or even a pretext) to recover prisoners, especially those not yet assimilated. In 1701, Father Marest, a Jesuit missionary at Michilimackinac, observed that for the Odawas, the return of "slaves ... was the most essential article of the peace agreement."

As it turned out, the delegates from the Great Lakes brought more than 30 Iroquois prisoners to exchange at the conference, but the leaders of the Five Nations came with only 12 French and two Native prisoners. All the ambassadors from the *pays d'en haut* complained to Callière about the Iroquois delinquency in this respect, even

Detail taken from the *Codex Canadiensis*, about 1675. Artist: Louis Nicolas. The Thomas Gilcrease Institute of American History and Art, Tulsa, 4726.7

threatening to take back their prisoners. Kondiaronk said, with bitterness: "My father … remember that you told us last fall that you wanted absolutely that we bring you all the Iroquois slaves who are among us. We obeyed you … I told you last year that it was better if they brought us our prisoners first, and now you see how it is, and how they have deceived us."

Callière paid heed, and during the farewell session with the Iroquois, he told them that the "[Native people] of the *pays d'en haut* … gave me your prisoners … Therefore I want to return them to you now, except for five who wanted to stay with the Hurons, so that you will all return home content with me, and I give you Sieur de Joncaire, as you wished, to bring back their people to me. Do not fail to redeem the error that you made by leaving them in your villages, and to overcome all the difficulties that you may encounter with the persons who have them, in order that I also may satisfy my allies … and convince them of your sincerity, so that beginning this winter you can hunt together in peace and without them mistrusting you. I ask you again, too, for the rest of my Frenchmen, so that these matters may be entirely concluded." The Iroquois complied with his request.

The Death of Kondiaronk

On 1 August, during a council between the French and the Huron-Petuns, Kondiaronk fell sick with a violent fever. "He received care very promptly," wrote Charlevoix, "especially because the governor general placed in him his main hope for the success of his great work … the general peace." "He first sat down on a folding chair," La Potherie reported. "They had a large comfortable chair brought so that he could rest and speak at his ease. He was given wine to fortify him. He asked to drink herbs, and they realized that he wanted maidenhair [a Native remedy]." Greatly weakened, Kondiaronk "revived somewhat and spoke in a rather listless voice for two hours." His words — "each different matter of which he spoke" — were given "infinite attention," and his compatriots "cheered him with voices that came from deep down." "We could not help but be touched by the eloquence with which he spoke, and admit at the same time that he was a man of merit," said La Potherie. His speech completed, Kondiaronk was carried in a chair to the hospital, where his condition continued to deteriorate. He died the following day at two o'clock in the morning.

Kondiaronk was carried back to his hut and carefully prepared for burial. "He was laid out on beaver pelts and a hat trimmed with a new red plume was placed on his head. He was covered with a large scarlet blanket," and beside him were placed a pot, a gun, and a sword. The varied origins of the deathbed objects expressed the mix of cultures in diplomatic meetings. Governor Callière and Intendant Champigny, bowing to Native ritual, "covered the deceased." The visit by the French representatives was followed by that of some 60 Iroquois, mostly

Senecas, who had asked Joncaire to walk at their head. They entered the hut of the Huron chief in a solemn procession. "When they came near the body, they formed a circle, and all sat down on the ground," except for a Seneca chief, Tonatakout, who continued to walk back and forth for a quarter of an hour, lamenting the death of Kondiaronk with tragic dignity. He was then replaced by Aouenano, a Seneca orator, who carried out the condolence ceremony, drying tears and opening throats to pour in "a sweet medicine" intended to restore the grieving Hurons. Displaying a wampum belt, Aouenano then declared to the Huron chiefs: "The sun is eclipsed today, it is the death of our brother Le Rat [Kondiaronk] that is the cause. We ask you to have the same spirit, the same sentiments as he had to hereafter form only one body, one kettle." They must continue to follow the path to peace that had been cleared by Kondiaronk.

The funeral took place on 3 August. The French wanted it to be magnificent, to let everyone know how deeply they felt the loss of this chief "who had been so commendable." The captain of the troops, Pierre de Saint-Ours, headed the procession, leading an escort of 60 soldiers. After them came 16 Huron warriors walking four by four, wearing long beaver pelts, their faces blackened as a sign of mourning and their guns pointed to the ground. Then came the members of the clergy, followed by six war chiefs carrying the flower-covered coffin, on which had been placed "a hat with a plume, a sword, and a gorget." Next came the family of the late chief — his brother and children — and many Huron and Odawa warriors. Madame de Champigny (the wife of the intendant), Philippe de Rigaud de Vaudreuil (the governor of Montreal), and all the officers of the general staff brought up the rear of the funeral procession. Two volleys of musket fire followed the celebration of the Catholic service, and then the body of Kondiaronk was buried in Notre Dame Church in Montreal.

Philippe de Rigaud, Marquis de Vaudreuil (ca. 1643–1725). Based on the original painting by Léopold Darangel. National Archives of Canada, Ottawa, C-100374

All the warriors and soldiers then fired a last round in turn. On the grave they put the inscription "Here lies Le Rat, chief of the Hurons." One hour after the funeral, Joncaire, leading some 50 Iroquois from La Montagne, brought "a wampum sun supported by two collars" to the Hurons and obtained their agreement not to leave the path of peace. Kondiaronk's death caused widespread grief and quite likely contributed to reconciliation among the conference participants.

In a classic tribute, not without a touch of ethnocentrism, La Potherie would write of Kondiaronk: "I cannot express to you ... the grief there was in his nation at the loss of a man so full of good qualities. It was difficult to have a more penetrating mind than his, and if he had been born French he would have had the character to govern the thorniest affairs of a prosperous state ... His words were like oracles ... He had the sentiments of a beautiful soul, and was a savage only in name."

THE "SAVAGE": A MATTER OF POINT OF VIEW

The word "savage" (from the Latin *silva*, "woods") was frequently used in references to Aboriginal people in the 17th and 18th centuries, as if to suggest that they were not as "civilized" as the Europeans, that they still belonged to the world of "nature." The encounter between Europeans and Native peoples was often presented, falsely, as an encounter between "civilization" and "savagery." In reality it was a meeting of two civilizations, each with its own specific technology, social organization, political structure, and philosophy. In the 17th century, each side had ethnocentric attitudes; each judged the other against the yardstick of its own culture. Native people, although they valued European goods, generally considered themselves superior to the French, looking down on them for their greed, their awkward gesticulating, and their inability to speak Native languages.

The General Assembly

At the general assembly, held on 4 August, the day after Kondiaronk's funeral, the peace agreement was ratified in a lavish ceremony. The French authorities, for whom luxury and pageantry were the preferred symbols of political power, made sure that it was an occasion worthy of the court of Louis XIV. "Everything was displayed for two days," reported La Potherie, and "many [Native] women were summoned to prepare [wampum belts]." To accommodate the general assembly, a huge rectangular arena, 43 metres long and 24 wide, had been created on a large plain south of Pointe-à-Callière (in present-day Old Montreal), between the town and the river. It was

Detail taken from *Historiæ Canadensis...* François Du Creux, Sebastian Cramoisy, Paris, 1664

bordered by a double enclosure of tree branches that formed a broad alley through which people could stroll. A hall 10 metres long, almost square, and covered with leaves, was built at one end of the arena.

On the appointed day, 2,000 to 3,000 people, perhaps more, filled this summery, rustic theatre. Whether they played leading roles or bit parts or were merely spectators, everyone was there to celebrate peace. Some 1,300 Native representatives arranged themselves by nation inside the enclosure "in a very orderly fashion," most of them sitting on the ground quietly smoking the peace pipe. Facing them were the French plenipotentiaries — Governor Callière, Intendant Champigny, and Governor of Montreal Vaudreuil — other officers, and scribes and interpreters. Many others were in attendance as well, for all of Montreal society was represented at this majestic assembly — the elite of the citizenry, people of the land, tradesmen, and the clergy. "People of quality" watched the proceedings from the covered hall, which was outfitted with tiers of seats. Dozens of French soldiers were placed around the palisade surrounding the area.

This colourful grand council, where Native chiefs "dressed in long hide robes," with painted faces and their heads adorned with feathers, rubbed shoulders with bewigged uniformed officers and ladies in their finery, was a spectacular expression of Canadian multiculturalism in its "colonial" form. In this context, the five interpreters, four of them Jesuits, provided an indispensable service. Father Garnier translated Callière's speeches for the Hurons, and theirs for the governor; Father Bigot interpreted for the Algonquins and Abenakis; Father Enjalran, for the Odawas; Father Bruyas, for the Iroquois; and finally, Nicolas Perrot, for most of the Great Lakes nations.

43

Governor Callière, with paper in hand, gave the first speech. "It is with extreme joy that I see all my children assembled here now," he said, "you Hurons, Sable Ottawas [Odawas], Kiskakons, Sinago Ottawas, Ottawas of the Fork, Saulteurs, Potawatomis, Sauks, Puants, Menominees, Foxes, Mascoutens, Miamis, Illinois, Amikwas, Nipissings, Algonquins, Timiskamings, Crees, *Gens des terres* ('inlanders') Kickapoos, people from the Sault and from La Montagne, Abenakis, and you the Iroquois nations, and having one and all placed your interests in my hands that I can have you all live in tranquillity. I therefore today ratify the peace agreement that we have made ... wishing that there be no more talk of the attacks made during the war, and I gather up again all your hatchets, and all your instruments of war, which I place with mine in a pit so deep that no one can take them back to disturb the tranquillity that I have re-established among my children, and I recommend to you when you meet to treat each other as brothers, and make arrangements for the hunt together so that there will be no quarrels among you ... I attach my words to the wampum belts I will give to each one of your nations in order that the elders may have them carried out by their young people. I invite you all to smoke this calumet that I will be the first to smoke, and to eat meat and broth that I have had prepared for you so that, like a good father, I have the satisfaction of seeing all my children united."

The interpreters, who had a copy of the speech, read it to the Native ambassadors, who shouted their approval. Callière, to please the Native delegates, had used many of their expressions — the pit in which the hatchets were buried, the wampum belts, the peace pipe, the broth in the kettle. He also observed traditional protocol, giving the delegates 31 wampum belts, which were hung on a large pole at the entry to the arena.

Then the Native orators — "the greatest orators in the world," according to one Jesuit priest — took the floor one after the other. Each ambassador was dressed and adorned with ceremonial care, and each spoke with majestic dignity. The Native peoples' love of theatricality, which equalled that of the French, was expressed through the use of pantomime, dance, and song as well as in the attention they paid to costumes, headdresses, and ornamentation. According to one Jesuit, the Native people "put their main glory in the adornment of their heads, especially their hair, whether long or short, according to the diversity of the nations." This concern for appearance led to innovations in dress during this important intercultural conference.

Hassaki, the Kiskakon chief, was the first Native orator to speak, indicating the pre-eminence of the Odawas within the French-Native alliance. Dressed in a "robe of beaver that hung to the ground" and displaying a wampum string and belt, he walked "in a majestic manner, leading four very handsome Iroquois, who had their eyes lowered" and whom he "had sit at his feet" before he began his oration. Later, after the Hurons, the other Odawas, and the Miamis had spoken, it was the Potawatomi chief Onanguicé's turn. According to Charlevoix, he wore a headdress made from a bison head, "with the horns hanging over his ears." The Ojibwa chief Ouabangué had also taken pains with his headdress: "He had red plumes around his head in the form of rays of light," noted La Potherie. The Algonquin chief, a "tall, remarkably well-built young man," was dressed "in the Canadian style" and his hair, in the shape of a crest, was decorated with red feathers that fell to his shoulders.

45

Painted deerskin, before 1796. Possibly Illinois. Artist unknown. Photographer: M. Delaplanche. Musée de l'Homme, Paris, France, 78.32.134

But Miskouensa, the orator for the Foxes, was undoubtedly the most theatrical. Accompanied by three Iroquois prisoners, he walked from "the far end of the enclosure" to the centre of the area. His face was painted red and he had covered his head with an old wig that was "heavily powdered and very badly combed." "He had made himself an ornament of it to follow the French manner ... and, wanting to show that he knew how to act, he saluted the Chevalier de Callière with it as if with a hat."

This scene, like those in which the French diplomats bowed to Native rituals, illustrates the creative aspect of the encounter and highlights the intensity of the cultural exchange. Each side was attempting to adapt to the other by mirroring its culture. Miskouensa, by adopting for his own purposes the representative signs (the wig) and the gestures of civility (the salute) of the European aristocrat, created an original costume that expressed the invention of a cosmopolitan "New World" as it flowered that summer in Montreal.

After Aouenano, representing the Iroquois, finished the round of speeches, Governor Callière had the peace treaty brought out, which the various chiefs signed by making their distinctive "marks." Then, one by one, over a long period, Callière, Champigny, Vaudreuil, and all the Native delegates, to "confirm this great alliance ... and to do it with all possible circumspection," smoked the big peace pipe that the Miami chief Chichicatalo had given the French governor.

The assembly ended with ceremonial dances and songs. Three Frenchmen distinguished themselves by making a very Native gesture: their faces animated, the movement of their bodies expressing the vehemence of their words, they marched rhythmically among the delegates who sat on the grass. The "Te Deum" was sung, and then all the participants were welcomed to share in the feast that had been prepared (three oxen boiled in 10 huge kettles, which La Potherie found "frugal for so many people"). Finally, to the sound of musket and artillery fire, the bonfire was lit, the closing note of this memorable day's festivities.

Callière organized the distribution of gifts during the final sessions, on 6 and 7 August. "The marks of esteem and friendship we had shown until then to all our allies," noted La Potherie, "would have made little impression on their minds if we had not at the same time done something more concrete and effective to acknowledge all the good services they had rendered to us. We therefore thought of giving them gifts, and had these prepared in the storehouses of the King."

THE TREATY SIGNATURES

The 1701 treaty of Montreal is a written document characteristic of European diplomatic culture. It made official, through pen and ink, the proposals put forth in the speeches. The French diplomats were therefore eager to have the Native chiefs validate the treaty with their "marks." It should be noted that when Native people signed treaties, they were not agreeing to what was actually written down, but rather to the words that had been orally delivered to them in their language by an interpreter. This sometimes led to misunderstandings, but that was not the case for the Montreal treaty. For one thing, the large number of participants and the scope of the negotiations excluded the possibility of there being specific agreements made with certain groups at the expense of the majority; secondly, the treaty did not involve any transfer of territory, a tricky business that often involved deception; and finally, since the French depended on alliances with the Native nations and had much to gain from a peace settlement, they would have wanted to make sure that all the participants, and not just some factions, were satisfied.

The treaty bears the "marks" or pictographs of close to 40 nations (compared to 13 on the treaty of September 1700). According to Father Charlevoix, "Each tribe [clan] bears the name of an animal, and the whole Nation also has its own, from which it takes its name and of which its mark is the symbol — if you wish, its coat of arms. These treaties are not signed otherwise than by drawing these figures, unless there are particular reasons for substituting others." Most of the symbols come from the animal world, both actual species and cosmological creatures (such as the thunderbird), but there are also human figures, plants, and objects such as the arrow, peace pipe, or scalp pole. Exactly what they signify or represent is difficult to determine, since signing treaties was new for Native people and a systematic practice had not developed. Nevertheless, whether he signed with a personal "mark" (individual totemism) or with the "mark" of a group (tribe, clan, moiety), the Native delegate committed himself on behalf of his nation.

Signing written documents in accordance with European convention was not a major cultural concession for Native people. They were accustomed to using pictographic symbols, which had spiritual value and sociological, mnemonic, and narrative functions. The pictographs on treaties are related to the traditional representational art that Native people in the Great Lakes region created on various surfaces: human skin or animal hide, bark, and rock. If there was a cultural concession on their part, it was that they had adapted to a new medium, paper.

THE NATIVE PARTICIPANTS IN THE GREAT PEACE OF MONTREAL

The Great Peace involved close to 40 Native nations. The following is a list of 37 of the participants (not all the signatures on the treaty have been identified).

1   The **Abenakis** of Acadia, represented by Meskouadoue. He may also have spoken for the Wabanaki Confederacy, which included the Penobscots, Passamaquoddys, Maliseets, and Mi'kmaqs, as well as the Abenakis of St. François.

2   The **Algonquins**.

3   The **Amikwas**, or Beaver nation, represented by Mahingan.

4   The **Crees**, or at least one of their bands.

5   The **Foxes** (or Outagamis), represented by Noro and Miskouensa.

6   The **Gens des terres** ("inlanders"), possibly a Cree band.

7   The **Huron-Petuns** (or Wyandots), represented by Kondiaronk, assisted by Quarante Sols, who spoke specifically for the Hurons of the St. Joseph River.

8-13   The **Illinois**, that is, the Kaskakias, Peorias, Tapouaros, Maroas, Coiracoentanons, and Moingwenas. In fact, because of the epidemic no Illinois ambassador reached Montreal. The Potawatomi chief Onanguicé represented them and may have signed for them, unless the Illinois pictographs found on the treaty were obtained earlier by the French officer Courtemanche during a diplomatic mission to the *pays d'en haut*.

14-18   The **Iroquois of the League**. At the head of the Onondaga, Seneca, Oneida, and Cayuga delegation in Montreal were the three Seneca leaders Tekanoet, Aouenano, and Tonatakout; the Onondaga sachem Ohonsiowanne; the Seneca chief Toarenguenion; the Cayuga Garonhiaron; and the Oneida Soueouon. They each signed the treaty for their respective nation. The Mohawks arrived in Montreal a few days later; they accepted the terms of the treaty but did not sign it.

19-20 The **Iroquois of Montreal**. Those from Kahnawake were represented by L'Aigle, and those of La Montagne, by Tsahouanhos.

21 The **Kickapoos**.

22 The **Mascoutens**, represented by Kiskatapi.

23 The **Menominees** (or Folles Avoines), represented by Paintage.

24-26 The **Miamis** from St. Joseph River, but also two other Miami nations — the Peanguichias and the Ouiatenons. All were represented by Chichicatalo.

27 The **Mississaugas**, represented by the Potawatomi chief Onanguicé on 4 August.

28 The **Nipissings**, represented by Onaganiouitak.

29-32 The **Odawas**, who were divided into four subgroups: the Sable Odawas, represented by Outoutagan (also known as Jean Le Blanc), orator, and by Kinongé ("Le Brochet"), signatory of the treaty; the Kiskakons, represented by Hassaki, orator, and by Kileouiskingié, signatory of the treaty; the Sinago Odawas, represented by Chingouessi, orator, and by Outaliboi, signatory of the treaty; and the Nassawaketons, or "Odawas of the Fork," represented by Elaouesse, orator and signatory.

33 The **Ojibwas** (Saulteurs), represented by Ouabangué.

49

34 The **Potawatomis**, represented by Onanguicé and seconded by Ouenemek.

35 The **Sauks**, represented by Coluby and sometimes by Onanguicé.

36 The **Timiskamings**.

37 The **Winnebagos** (or Puants).

Ratification De la Paix

faitte au mois de septembre, dernier, entre La Colonie de
Canada, Les Sauvages ses alliéz, et les iroquois dans une
assemblée generalle des chefs de chacune de ces nations
convoquéz par monsieur le Chevalier de Callieres
gouverneur et Lieutenant general pour le Roy en la
nouvelle france,

A Montreal le quatrième aoust 1701

Comme il ny avoit icy l'année dernière que des
deputéz des hurons et des outaouacs lorsque ie fis la paix
avec les Iroquois pour moy et tous mes alliéz, il ung eay quil
estoit necessaire d'envoyer le Sieur de Courtemanche,
et le Père ... Anjalran, chéz toutes les autres nations mes
alliéz, qui estoient absentes pour leur apprendre ce qui
sestoit passé, et les inviter à descendre des chefs de
chacune avec les prisonniers iroquois quils avoient affin
d'escouter tous ensemble ma parolle,

Jay une extreme ioye de voir icy presentement tous mes
enfans assembléz, vous hurons, outaouacs du Sable,
Kiskakons, outaouacs Sinago, nation de la fourche,
Sauteurs, Poutëatamis, Sakis, puants, folles avoines, renars,
mascoutins, Miamis, Ilinois, amikois, nepisinques, algonquins
Temiskamingues, Cristinaux, gens des terres, Kikapoux, gens
du Sault, de la montagne, Abenakis, et vous nations iroquoises,
et que m'ayant remis les uns, et les autres vos interests
entre les mains ie puisse vous faire vivre tous En
tranquilité, ie ratiffie dont auiourd'huy la paix que nous
avons faitte au mois d'aoust dernier voulant quil ne soit
plus parlé de tous les coups, faits pendant la guerre, et
ie me saisy de nouveau de toutes vos haches, et de tous vos
autres instruments de guerre, que ie mets avec les miens
dans une fosse sy proffonde que personne ne puisse les
reprendre, pour troubler la tranquilité que ie restablis
parmy mes Enfans, en vous recommandant lorsque vous
vous rencontrerez de vous traiter comme freres, et de vous
accomoder ensemble pour la chasse, de manière qu'il n'arrive

aucune Brouillerie les uns les autres, et pour que cette
paix ne puisse estre troublée, ie repete ce que i'ay desja dit
dans le traité que nous avons fait, que s'il arrivoit que
quelqu'un de mes enfans en frapat un autre, celuy qui aura
esté, frapé ne se vangera point, ny par luy ny par aucun
de sa part, mais il viendra me trouver pour que ie luy en
fasse, faire raison, vous declarant que si l'offensant
refusoit d'en faire une satisfaction raisonnable, ie me ioindre
avec mes autres alliéz à l'offensé pour l'y contraindre
ce qui ne croit pas qui puisse arriver, par l'obeissance
que me doivent mes enfans qui se ressouviendront de ce que
nous arrestons presentement ensemble, et pour qu'ils ne
puissent l'oublier, j'attache mes parolles aux colliers que
ie vais donner a chacune de vos nations affin que les
anciens les fassent executer par leurs jeunes gens, ie vous
invite tous a fumer dans ce calumet de paix ou ie commence
le premier, et a manger de la viande, et du bouillon que ie
vous fais preparer pour que i'aye comme un bon père
la satisfaction de voir tous mes enfans reunis,

Je garderay ce calumet qui m'a esté presenté par les
miamis affin que ie puisse vous faire fumer quand
vous viendrez me voir;

Après que toutes les nations cy dessus eurent entendu
ce que monsieur le Chevalier de Callieres leur dit, ils
respondirent comme il suit,

Le Chef des Kiskakons

Je n'ay pas voulu manquer mon père ayant sçû que vous
me demandiéz les prisonniers des Iroquois, a vous les amener
en voila quatre que ie vous presente pour en faire ce qu'il
vous plaira, C'est avec cette porcelaine que ie les ay deliéz,
et voicy un calumet que ie presente aux iroquois pour fumer
ensemble quand nous nous rencontrerons, ie me resjouy de
ce que vous avez uny la terre qui estoit bouleversée, et ie
... souscris volontiers à tout ce que vous avez fait;

Les Iroquois

Nous voila assembléz nostre père comme vous l'aviéz
souhaitté; vous plantates l'année dernière un arbre de paix

Reproduction of the Great Peace of Montreal Treaty, August 4, 1701.
Archives nationales de France, Paris

Et vous y mittes des racines et des feuilles pour que nous y puissions
a labry, nous esperons presentement que tout le monde entend
ce que vous dites, qu'on ne touchera point a cet arbre, pour nous
nous vous assurons, par ces quatre colliers que nous sçaurons
tout ce que vous auez reglé, nous vous presentons deux prisonniers
que voicy et nous vous rendrons les autres que nous auons, Nous
esperons aussy presentement que les portes sont ouvertes pour
la paix, qu'on nous renuoyera le reste des nostres,

Les hurons,

Nous voila icy comme vous l'auez demandé, nous vous presentons
douze prisonniers, dont cinq veullent retourner auec nous, pour
les sept autres vous en ferez ce qu'il vous plaira, nous vous
remercions de la paix que vous nous auez procuré et nous
la ratifions auec ioye,

Jean le blanc outaouac du Sable,

Je vous ay obey mon pere aussy tost que vous m'auez demandé
en vous ramenant deux prisonniers dont vous estes le maistre
quand vous m'auez commandé d'aller a la guerre ie l'ay fait,
et a present que vous me le deffendez iy obey, ie vous demande
mon pere par ce collier que les iroquois veillent mon corps
qui est chez eux, et qu'il me le renuoyent (C'est a dire les gens
de sa nation)

Sangouessy outaouac Sinago,

Je n'ay pas voulu manquer a vos ordres mon pere quoique ie
n'aye point de prisonniers, Cependant voila vne femme et vn
enfant que i'ay racheptés dont vous ferez ce qu'il vous plaira,
et voila vn calumet que ie donne aux iroquois pour fumer come
freres quand nous nous rencontrerons,

Chichicatalo Chef des Miamis

Je vous ay obey mon pere en vous ramenant 8 prisonniers Iroquois
pour en faire ce qu'il vous plaira, si i'auois eu des Canots, ie vous
en aurois amené d'auantage, quoy que ie ne voye point icy des
miens qui sont chez les iroquois, ie vous rameneray ce qui m'en
reste, si ie le souhaite, ou ie leur ouuriray les portes pour qu'ils
s'en retournent,

Onanguissé pour Les Sakis,

Je ne fais qu'vn mesme corps auec vous mon Pere, voila Vn
prisonnier Iroquois que i'auois fait a la guerre, souffrez qu'en vous
le presentant ie luy donne vn calumet pour emporter chez les
Iroquois et fumer quand nous nous rencontrerons, ie vous remercie

De ce que vous eclairez le soleil qui estoit obscur depuis la guerre,

Onanguissé Chef des Potrouatamis,

Je ne vous feray point vn long discours mon pere, ie n'ay plus que
deux prisonniers que ie mets a vos deux costez pour en faire ce qu'il
vous plaira, voila vn calumet que ie vous presente pour que vous
le gardiez, ou que vous le donniez a ces deux prisonniers afin
qu'ils fument dedans chez eux, ie suis tousiours prest a vous
obeir iusqu'a la mort,

Misgensa Chef Ontagamis,

Je n'ay point de prisonniers a vous rendre mon pere, mais ie
vous remercie du beaujour que vous donnez a toute la Terre
par la paix, pour moy ie ne perdray iamais cette clarté,

Les Maskoutins

Je ne vous amene point d'Esclaue iroquois par ce que il n'ay pas
esté en party contre eux depuis quelque tems, m'estant amusé a
faire la guerre a d'autres nations, mais ie suis venu pour vous obeir
et vous remercier de la paix que vous nous procurez,

Les folles auoines

Je suis seullement venu mon pere pour vous obeir et
embrasser la paix que auez faite entre les Iroquois et nous,

Les Sauteurs et les Puants

Je vous aurois amené mon pere des Esclaues iroquois sy
i'en auois eu, voulant vous obeir en ce que vous m'ordonnerez,
ie vous remercie de la clarté que vous nous donnez et ie souaite
quelle dure, Les Nepissingues

Les Nepissingues

Je n'ay pas voulu manquer a me rendre icy comme les autres
pour escouter vostre voix, i'auois vn prisonnier iroquois que
l'année passée que ie vous ay rendu, voila vn calumet que
ie vous presente pour le donner aux iroquois si vous le souaitez
affin de fumer ensemble quand nous nous rencontrerons,

Les Algonquins

Je n'ay point de prisonniers a vous rendre mon pere, l'algonquin
est vn de vos enfans qui a tousiours esté a vous, et qui y sera
tant qu'il viura, ie prie le maistre de la vie que ce que vous
faites aujourd'huy dure,

La Mikois

N'ayant point d'autre volonté que la vostre, j'obey a ce que
vous venez de faire,

51

52

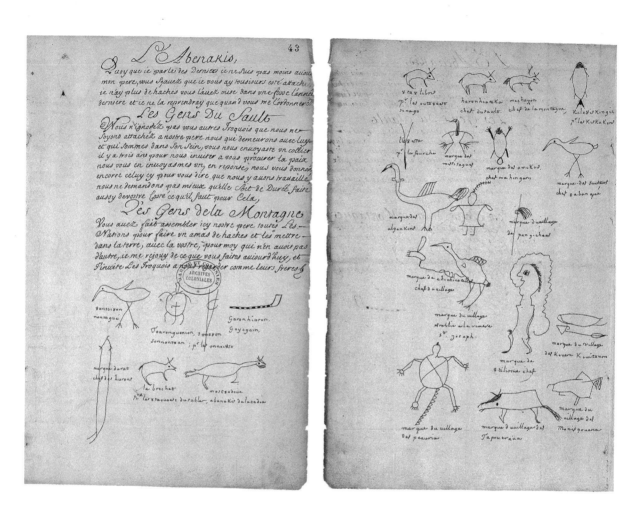

L'Abenakis,

Quoy que ie parle des Derniers ie ne suis pas moins auiourd'huy
mon pere, vous sçauez que ie vous ay tousiours esté attaché,
ie n'ay plus de haches vous l'auez mise dans une fosse l'année
derniere et ie ne la reprendray que quand vous me l'ordonnerez.

Les Gens Du Sault

Vous n'ignorez pas vous autres Iroquois que nous ne
soyons attachez a nostre pere nous qui demeurons auec luy
et qui sommes dans son sein, vous nous envoyaste un collier
il y a trois ans pour nous inuiter a vous procurer la paix
nous vous en envoyasmes un, en reponse, nous vous donnons
encore celuy cy pour vous dire que nous y auons trauaillé,
nous ne demandons pas mieux qu'elle soit de Durée, faites
aussy de vostre Costé ce qu'il faut pour Cela.

Les Gens de la Montagne

Vous auez fait assembler icy nostre pere toutes Les
Nations pour faire un amas de haches et les mettre
dans la terre, auec la vostre, pour moy qui n'en auois pas
d'autre, ie me rejouy de ce que vous faites auiourd'huy, et
i'inuite Les Iroquois à nous regarder comme leurs freres.

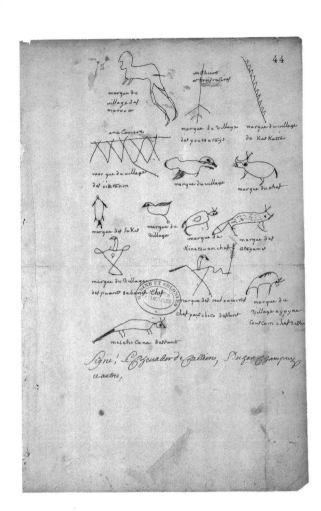

marque du
village des
marouas

un Chicot
et trois racines

marque du Village
des poutsataiys

marque du village
de Kaskatta

une Careve

marque du village
des oskitanon

marque du village

marque du chef

marque des Sakis

marque du
village

marque de
Kinatsuan chef

marque des
atygamis

marque du village
des puant Sabonya Chef

marque des mal oumins
chef pas checo dessant

marque du
village nypyna
Coutam chef dessant

milchi cana dessant

Signé, le Chevalier de Callaire, St Organ Champuis
et autres,

Part Three

THE MONTREAL AGREEMENT

When the conference was over, the delegates from the *pays d'en haut*, still weakened by the "cold," headed back home. Before leaving Montreal, Outoutagan addressed Callière on their behalf: "Pray to the Master of Life to preserve us on our voyage, to dispel our stomach-aches and headaches, so that our relatives will see us all happy." The next day, the Iroquois also bid farewell. Montreal returned to normal, but the conference would leave its imprint on all parties to the great peace.

The Neutrality of the Iroquois League

In signing the Montreal treaty, the Iroquois League did not capitulate, but it did accept peace terms, dictated by the French and their allies, that it had rejected a few years earlier. Weakened militarily, the League succeeded nevertheless in advancing its own interests, both in Montreal and in Albany, where it negotiated a renewal of the Covenant Chain with the New York authorities at the same time.

THE ALBANY AGREEMENTS

From 12 to 21 July 1701, 33 sachems from the Iroquois League, led by leaders of the pro-English faction, met with John Nanfan, the new governor of New York. Their goal was to clarify the terms of the Covenant Chain in light of the treaty about to be signed in Montreal. The Iroquois had to strike a delicate balance, confirming the alliance with the English in spite of the peace treaty with the French. Although the economic alliance was easily renewed, the military alliance posed problems. While holding to the principle of neutrality, the Iroquois expressed the hope that "if a war broke out between us [the Five Nations] and the French, ... you [the English] will be ready to assist us and defend us."

The Montreal treaty established the neutrality of the Five Nations. On 7 August, Callière had told the Iroquois delegates: "I have informed you ... that if war begins again between us [the French] and the English ... you should not think of becoming involved. I repeat to you again ... by this [wampum] collar, that in the event that war comes, you should remain peacefully smoking on your mats, without taking any part in our troubles." In neutralizing the Iroquois, Callière had altered the balance of power between the colonial empires: he had deprived New York of its front line of combatants and had made Iroquoia a valuable buffer zone.

Neutrality, however, also fulfilled some Iroquois goals — specifically, for the faction led by Teganissorens. Full political independence with respect to the French and English allowed them to play the two against each other when it suited their interests. While their economic alliance with the English was confirmed, they gained access to French markets to obtain European goods, whether in Fort Frontenac, Detroit (founded earlier in the summer of 1701 by a captain of the marine, Lamothe Cadillac), or Montreal. Neutrality also provided the Iroquois with guarantees regarding hunting territories and helped ease internal tensions within the League. The Great Peace also benefited the "settled" Iroquois living along the St. Lawrence. They became middlemen in the trade between Albany and Montreal.

The French-Native Alliance Confirmed

Callière — and through him Louis XIV — had good reason to be satisfied. The treaty of 1701 confirmed the French multilateral alliance with the nations of the *pays d'en haut*. In hosting the peace negotiations and acting as intermediary between the western allies and the Iroquois, the governor gave official status to his position as arbitrator and mediator in New France. "If it happened that one of my children struck another," proclaimed Callière on 4 August, "the one who was attacked should not take revenge ... but he should come to find me so that I can have justice done for him ... [and] if the offending party refused to make reasonable satisfaction, I and

my other allies will join with the offended party to compel him, which I do not believe would happen, because of the obedience owed to me by my children, who will remember again what we are deciding now together." This clause allowed the French governor to consolidate his central position within the alliance. His power as a mediator, however, was not absolute, since it derived from Native tradition and the alliance was an association of sovereign nations, even though the French could be said to dominate.

The 1701 conference was intended to strengthen French influence in the *pays d'en haut* by reducing French-Native tensions. Callière accepted reparations (in the form of gifts or prisoners) from chiefs eager to have their warriors forgiven for robbing *coureurs des bois*. He also attempted to stop hostilities between his allies. But paradoxically, the original French-Native alliance emerged from the Great Peace somewhat weakened. The Great Lakes nations could now be reconciled with both the Iroquois and Albany. They had no intention of leaving the comfortable bosom of Onontio's French alliance, but they hoped to manoeuvre the French into being more generous in trade and they planned to take advantage, on occasion, of the attractive New York market.

Huron Couple, Quebec, about 1750-1775. Artist unknown. Philéas Gagnon Collection, Ville de Montréal, Gestion de documents et archives, BM7, 42500 (034-02-04-01)

Conclusion

The treaty of Montreal was an important event in the history of New France. Unlike many of the treaties signed in the previous century, this peace would be long lasting. Even though the Five Nations, under the influence of the British, came close to attacking the French during the imperial wars of the 18th century, their hostility towards Canada was largely a thing of the past and the principle of neutrality was respected. The peace settlement was an enormous relief for all the French colonists, particularly the inhabitants of Montreal, who had been living under threat of attack since the Iroquois raid on Lachine in 1689. The Great Peace also put an end to the French-Native military expeditions into Iroquois territory.

With the treaty of 1701 came a reorientation of Five Nations diplomacy. The League adopted, for example, a policy of alliance with the nations of the *pays d'en haut.* Of course, the Tree of Peace was sometimes uprooted in the Great Lakes region, since war was often an individual undertaking, waged by careless young men in defiance of the wisdom of the elders. But the confrontations of the 18th century were limited to a few skirmishes. The "Iroquois Wars" in Canada thus ended in 1701.

The Great Peace, however, did not mean the end of traditional Native warfare. The peace agreements made and alliances formed by Aboriginal nations were never universal. A nation always had an enemy to fight, whether neighbour or distant foe. The allies in the *pays d'en haut* had no intention of making peace with both the Iroquois and the Sioux, and thus the latter remained their enemy. Moreover, starting in 1712, a long war was waged by the French and their allies against the Foxes, Mascoutens, and Kickapoos. As for the Iroquois, according to La Potherie, they "never made peace with any nation without planning to make war elsewhere." They had not renounced war; rather, they now chose to avoid fighting too many enemies at the same time.

The Great Peace of Montreal is a powerful illustration of the effectiveness of the French-Native alliance. It was the crowning achievement of a certain form of colonialism based not on agricultural expansion and settlement but on alliance with the indigenous peoples and adaptation (largely tactical) to their political customs. The peace agreement of 1701 thus appeared to mark the success of French colonization in North America. Such, however, was not the case. Although the network of alliances between the Native nations and the French would last until 1760, the demographic imbalance between New France and the British colonies was already making itself felt in 1701.

Finally, the Montreal conference was a manifestation of a historical reality of which the celebration of its tercentenary is a powerful reminder. Forty nations came together as equals to sign a peace treaty, proof of France's de facto recognition of the independence and sovereignty of the Native nations. The Aboriginal peoples of the *pays d'en haut*, those of the Atlantic region, and the Iroquois of the League and of the Christian villages were all able to promote their own interests at the Montreal conference. They were not passive victims, but rather important actors in the history of North America. Many Native chiefs worked with the French in drawing up the treaty, and the conference saw the triumph of Native diplomatic traditions in the "colonial" arena. Native peoples, along with Europeans — French and English — emerge as co-founders of Quebec and Canada.

If 300 years ago 40 disparate nations could brave the dangers of travel and disease to gather together to put an end to their disputes, perhaps we have reason to hope that today's problems between Native peoples and North Americans of European descent are not as insurmountable as they may sometimes appear.

Headdress, late 18th or early 19th century. Possibly Iroquois, maker unknown. David Ross McCord Collection, McCord Museum, Montreal, M182

Chronology

Events Leading up to the Signing of the Great Peace of Montreal in 1701

1603

Alliance formed at Tadoussac between the French, the Montagnais, the Algonquins, and the Maliseets

1608

Founding of the town of Quebec by Samuel de Champlain

1609

Beginning of the French-Huron alliance

1609, 1610, 1615

French-Huron campaigns against the Iroquois

1642

Founding of Montreal

1645

Trois-Rivières peace treaty between the Mohawks, the French, and the Aboriginal allies of the French (Hurons, Algonquins, Montagnais, and Attikameks)

1648-1650

Destruction of the villages of Huronia by the Iroquois and dispersal of the Huron people

1666

Campaigns by the French Carignan-Salières regiment against the Mohawks

1667

General peace agreement in Quebec between the French, their Aboriginal allies, and the Iroquois; Jesuits settle among the Iroquois; Iroquois begin settling near Montreal

1677

Albany treaties inaugurating the Covenant Chain as a multilateral alliance of English colonies with several Aboriginal nations under the supervision of the Iroquois

1684

Joseph-Antoine Le Febvre de La Barre's failed campaign against the Senecas; La Famine peace treaty

1687

Jacques René de Brisay de Denonville's campaign against the Senecas

1689

Iroquois attack on Lachine

1693

French-Aboriginal campaign against the Mohawks

1694

Quebec conference between the French, their Aboriginal allies, and the Iroquois

1696

Campaigns by the French and their Aboriginal allies against the Onondagas and the Oneidas; trading posts closed in the *pays d'en haut* (the Great Lakes region)

1697

Treaty of Ryswick between France and England

1698

November: Death of Louis de Buade de Frontenac; appointment of Louis Hector de Callière as governor general of New France

1699

January: Onondaga-Oneida delegation in Montreal

March: Onondaga-Oneida delegation in Montreal

September: Onondaga delegation in Montreal

1700

July: Onondaga-Seneca delegation in Montreal

August: French-Iroquois conference in Onondaga

September: Peace agreement between the French, the Huron-Petuns, the Odawas, the Abenakis, the Montreal Iroquois, and the Five Nations Iroquois

1701

Winter: Diplomatic mission by Augustin Le Gardeur de Courtemanche and Father Enjalran to the *pays d'en haut*

May: Iroquois delegation in Montreal

June: French delegation in Onondaga

June-July: Founding of Detroit by Lamothe Cadillac

July: English-Iroquois conference in Albany

21-22 July: Aboriginal delegations arrive in Kahnawake

23 July to 7 August: General peace conference in Montreal

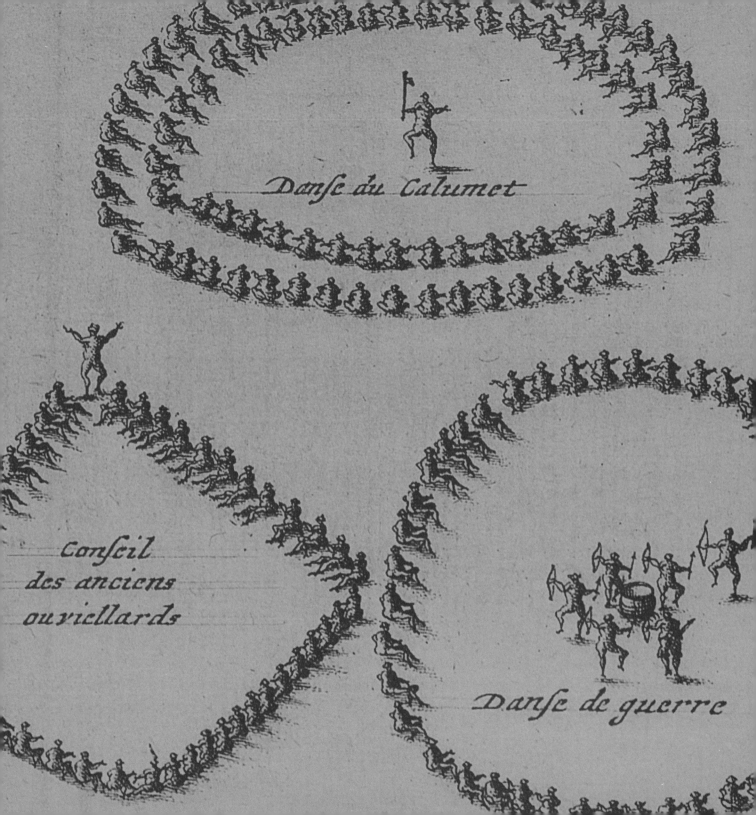

Danſe du Calumet

Conſeil
des anciens
ou vieillards

Danſe de guerre

Aboriginal Dignitaries

Aouenano

Aouenano was the civil chief of the Senecas, a leader of the pro-French faction of the Iroquois League, and one of the Iroquois delegation's principal orators (with Tekanoet) at the Montreal peace conference in 1701. He and Tonatakout led the Iroquois condolence ceremony for Kondiaronk.

Aradgi

An Onondaga chief, Aradgi played an important role in convincing his people to accept the terms of peace dictated by the French. However, he did not attend the Montreal conference in 1701.

Chichicatalo

Chief and ambassador of the Miamis of the St. Joseph River, Chichicatalo was one of the leading figures at the Great Peace of Montreal in 1701. He offered the French governor a peace pipe, which the plenipotentiaries smoked at the August 4 meeting.

Chingouessi

A Sinago Odawa chief, Chingouessi participated in the 1701 conference in Montreal.

Hassaki

Hassaki was an Odawa Kiskakon chief and the first Native orator to speak at the general assembly on 4 August 1701, indicating the pre-eminence of the Odawas among the Native groups within the French-Native alliance. It was Kileouiskingié, however, who signed the treaty on behalf of the Kiskakons.

Kinongé, or Le Brochet ("The Pike")

Chief of the Sable Odawas, Kinongé was signatory to the two Montreal treaties (1700 and 1701), but it was Outoutagan who apparently had the greatest influence among the Sable Odawas.

Kondiaronk, or Le Rat ("The Muskrat") (about 1649-1701)

Kondiaronk was chief and representative of the Huron-Petuns, and the principal Native architect of the Great Peace of Montreal. He had all the qualities of a leader — political genius, skill as a warrior, and unparalleled eloquence as an orator. Protective of his people's interests, he wished above all to prevent a separate peace between the French and the Iroquois. In 1700-1701, he endeavoured to convince all his allies to make their way to Montreal. He died during the peace conference as a result of a "violent fever." Grandiose funeral arrangements were organized in his honour.

Koutaoiliboe

This Odawa Kiskakon chief took part in the 1700 Montreal peace conference.

Le Baron

Chief of the Huron-Petuns, Le Baron led the anti-French Huron faction around 1695-1697, and negotiated with both the Iroquois and the English. He apparently wanted the Wyandots and the Odawas to make peace with the Iroquois independently of the French, and to join the diplomatic and trade network of the Covenant Chain.

Massias

An Iroquois chief of La Montagne.

Miskouensa

Miskouensa was a Fox orator in Montreal in 1701. At the assembly on August 4, his face was painted red and he wore a European-style powdered wig.

Noro, or Le Porc-épic ("The Porcupine")

Noro was chief of the Foxes at the peace conference in 1701.

Onanguicé

Chief of the Potawatomis, Onanguicé opposed the return of Iroquois prisoners by the Native peoples of the *pays d'en haut.* He spoke on behalf of most of the western nations at the 1701 conference.

Otachété

An Iroquois chief from Kahnawake.

Ouabangué

An Ojibwa chief, Ouabangué participated in the 1701 peace conference. He offered Noro a gift on behalf of his people to erase the memory of the killing of one of the Foxes.

Ouenemek

A chief of the St. Joseph River Potawatomis, Ouenemek took part (with Onanguicé) in the Montreal peace conference in 1701.

Outoutagan, or Jean Le Blanc

A Sable Odawa chief, Outoutagan participated in separate negotiations between the Iroquois and the Odawas around 1694-1695, then joined the French side. He took part in the peace conference in 1701, intent on defending his people's interests, and opposing in particular the sale of alcohol to his allies.

Quarante Sols, or Michipichy

In 1701, Quarante Sols was chief of the St. Joseph River Hurons. Either an Iroquois by birth, or a former prisoner of the Iroquois, he claimed to have played an important role in rallying the Native peoples from the *pays d'en haut* to the 1701 peace accord.

Teganissorens

A chief of the Onondaga nation, Teganissorens promoted the political autonomy of the Five Nations. In 1700-1701, he was the principal strategist for the League's diplomatic efforts, opting for a position of neutrality between the two European empires.

Tegayesté

An Iroquois chief from Kahnawake, Tegayesté served as ambassador for Frontenac among the Onondagas.

Tekanoet

Tekanoet was an important chief of the Seneca nation. At the Montreal peace conference in 1701, he was welcomed by Joncaire before he made his way to greet Governor Callière.

Tonatakout

Tonatakout was a Seneca chief. He spoke on behalf of the four western nations of the Iroquois League. A participant in the 1701 conference, he presided (with Aouenano) over the Iroquois condolence ceremony for Kondiaronk.

EUROPEAN DIGNITARIES

Bigot, Vincent (1649-1720)

A Jesuit missionary and founder of the mission at Pentagouet in Acadia, Bigot was also responsible for maintaining the alliance with the Abenakis. He was official interpreter for the Abenakis and the Algonquins at the Montreal conference in 1701.

Bruyas, Jacques (1635-1712)

Bruyas was a Jesuit missionary among the Oneidas in the 1660s, and among the Mohawks in the 1670s, and then took charge of the mission at Sault St. Louis (Kahnawake) after 1679. Bruyas helped to convince the Five Nations to send representatives to Montreal in 1701, where he acted as interpreter.

Cadillac, Antoine Laumet, known as de Lamothe Cadillac (1658-1730)

A captain in the marine and then commander of Michilimackinac, Cadillac founded the first colony at Detroit. He became increasingly despotic, extorting money through the sale of alcohol, taxes, and bribes, earning the enmity of colonists and Native peoples alike, and jeopardizing the French network of Native alliances. Cadillac was removed from his position in 1710 and sent to Louisiana as governor. He was recalled to France in 1717.

Callière, Louis Hector de (1648-1703)

As governor of Montreal from 1684 to 1698, Callière fortified the city and organized numerous raids against the Iroquois. At Frontenac's death (1698), he became governor general of the colony, and presided over the Montreal conference of 1701. Sometimes disliked for his severe and authoritarian manner, Callière was nevertheless a devoted and competent officer, at ease in both military and diplomatic matters.

Champigny, Jean Bochart de (about 1645-1720)

Intendant of New France from 1686 to 1702, Champigny assisted Denonville in the campaign against the Senecas (1687). He took an active role in the organization of the peace conference in 1701.

Champlain, Samuel de (about 1570-1635)

Draftsman, geographer, explorer, Champlain founded the town of Quebec in 1608 and was commander of New France from 1629 to 1635. He initiated the fur trade in Canada, and diplomatic and economic alliances with the Montagnais, the Algonquins, and the Hurons.

Charlevoix, Pierre-François-Xavier de (1682-1761)

A Jesuit historian, Charlevoix undertook two brief trips to America in 1705 and 1720. Although not present at the conference in 1701, he provided a narrative of the events in his history of New France.

Courtemanche, Augustin Le Gardeur de (1663-1717)

Born in Quebec, Courtemanche was a soldier and diplomat in the service of the colonial authorities. As an expert in Native relations, he was sent on various western missions, and in 1700 travelled to the Great Lakes region to persuade the allies to take part in the peace conference of 1701.

Denonville, Jacques-René de Brisay, Marquis de (1637-1710)

Governor of New France from 1685 to 1689, Denonville organized a military expedition against the Senecas in 1687. As the war dragged on, however, he was forced to order the evacuation of the Niagara and Frontenac forts in 1689. He was recalled to France that same year, and succeeded as governor by Frontenac.

Enjalran, Jean (1639-1718)

A Jesuit missionary among the Odawas, Father Enjalran was sent by Callière to Michilimackinac to invite the western nations to take part in the peace conference. In 1701, Enjalran translated Governor Callière's speeches for the Odawas and the Algonquins.

Frontenac, Louis de Buade de Frontenac et de Palluau (1622-1698)

Twice governor general of New France (1672-1682 and 1689-1698), Frontenac organized military campaigns against the Iroquois, and promoted the creation of new trading posts in the Great Lakes region, in defiance of directives from Versailles. An exceptional diplomat, he earned the respect of the Native ambassadors with whom he dealt and who called him "father." Despite several attempts, Frontenac failed to secure a peace with the Iroquois before his death in 1698, and it was his successor, Callière, who finally concluded the peace in 1701.

Garnier, Julien (1643-1730)

Garnier was a Jesuit missionary in Iroquoia. Fluent in several Native languages, particularly Algonquin and Huron and the five Iroquois dialects, Garnier served as an interpreter at the Montreal conference in 1701.

Joncaire, Louis Thomas Chabert de (1670-1739)

A French diplomat in Canada, Joncaire was adopted by the Senecas. He persuaded the Iroquois to participate in the Montreal peace conference in 1701, where his intimate knowledge of Iroquois protocol permitted him to play a predominant role.

La Barre, Joseph-Antoine Le Febvre de (1622-1688)

Governor of New France (1682-1685), La Barre undertook an expedition against the Iroquois in 1684, but his starved and sickly troops forced him to negotiate a precarious peace with the Iroquois. He was recalled to France in 1685.

Lahontan, Louis-Armand de Lom d'Arce, baron de (1666-1716)

Lahontan was a writer and officer in the marine. He took part in several expeditions against the Iroquois (La Barre, Denonville). Returning to France in 1693, he produced several histories of the colony and of the Aboriginal peoples.

La Potherie, Claude-Charles Le Roy, known as Bacqueville de la Potherie (1663-1736)

La Potherie was chief writer in the marine, commissary, then comptroller of the marine and of the fortifications of New France. He was posted to Canada for only three years, from 1698 to 1701. Although La Potherie played no official role in the negotiations of the Great Peace, he was present at the signing of the treaty and left meticulously recorded descriptions of Native protocol.

Louis XIV (1638-1715)

Callière signed the treaty of the Great Peace of Montreal in 1701 in the name of King Louis XIV of France, who reigned from 1643 to 1715. In 1663, Louis XIV declared the colony a royal province, and established, with his minister Colbert, a policy to settle the territory. It was his father, Louis XIII (1601-1643), who had first given a charter in 1627 to the 100 associates of the Company of New France, granting them exclusive right to the fur trade.

Maricourt, Paul Le Moyne de (1663-1704)

Born in Montreal, Maricourt was a soldier and diplomat. Adopted by the Onondagas, he was an effective agent for Frontenac and then Callière in negotiations with the Five Nations. In 1701, he acted as host to several Iroquois ambassadors, and likely played an important role in the discussions and festivities.

Montmagny, Charles Huault de (1583-1653)

Montmagny was the first governor of New France (1636-1648). The Aboriginal peoples called him Onontio ("Great Mountain"), the literal Huron-Iroquois translation of his name. In 1645, he signed a treaty with the Mohawks.

Perrot, Nicolas (1644-1717)

Perrot was an explorer, diplomat, *coureur des bois*, and interpreter. From 1670 to 1701, he was New France's most valuable agent in the Great Lakes region. He was entrusted with maintaining the colony's Native alliances, which he pursued alongside his fur-trading activities. On several occasions, he pushed the western nations (Odawas, Huron-Petuns, etc.) to wage war against the Five Nations. In 1701, he translated Callière's orations for the western delegates.

Saint-Ours, Pierre de (1640-1724)

A military officer, Saint-Ours took part in the 1666 expeditions against the Iroquois. In 1701, he headed the funeral procession for Kondiaronk, leading an escort of 60 soldiers.

Vaudreuil, Philippe de Rigaud de (1643-1725)

A musketeer of the French king, then commander of the troops in New France, Vaudreuil played an active role in the raids against the Iroquois in the 1690s. He became governor of Montreal in 1699 and, with the death of Callière in 1703, governor general of the colony.

Misgensa Chef Ontaganis,

Je n'ay point de prisonniers a vous rendre mon pere, mais
vous remercie du beau jour que vous donnéz a toute la te
par la paix, pour moy ie ne perdray iamais cette clart

Les Maskoutins

Je ne vous amene point d'Esclaue iroquois par ce que il v
sté en party contre eux depuis quelque tems, m'estant am
aire la guerre a d'autres nations, mais ie suis venu pour
t vous remercier de la paix que vous nous procuréz,

Les folles auoines.

e suis seullement venu mon pere pour vous obeir et
mbrasser la paix que auéz faite entre les Iroquois et n

Les Sauteurs et les Puants

Je vous aurois amené mon pere des Esclaues iroquoi
s'en auois eu, voullant vous obeir en ce que vous m'ordon
ie vous remercie de la clarté que vous nous donnéz et ie
uelle dure, Les Nepissingues

Les Nepissingues

Je n'ay pas voulu manquer a me rendre icy comme le
pour écouster vostre voix, i'auois vn prisonnier iroq

Further Reading

THREE AUTHORS OF THE PERIOD

Charlevoix, P. François Xavier de. *Histoire et description générale de la Nouvelle-France, avec le journal historique d'un voyage fait par ordre du Roi dans l'Amérique septentrionale*. Éditions Élysée, Ottawa, 1976 (1744), 3 vol.

Lahontan, Louis Armand de Lom d'Arce, baron de. *Œuvres complètes*. R. Ouellet and A. Beaulieu, eds. Presses de l'Université de Montréal, Montreal, 1990, 2 vol.

La Potherie, Le Roy Claude-Charles Le Roy [known as Bacqueville de la Potherie]. *Histoire de l'Amérique septentrionale*. Nion fils, Quai des Augustins, Paris, 1753 (1722), 4 vol.

SOME BOOKS AND ARTICLES ON NEW FRANCE AND ABORIGINAL PEOPLES

Aquila, Richard. *The Iroquois Restoration: Iroquois Diplomacy on the Colonial Frontier, 1701-1754*. Wayne State University Press, Detroit, 1983.

Beaulieu, Alain. *Les autochtones du Québec: des premières alliances aux revendications contemporaines*. Musée de la civilisation and Éditions Fides, Quebec, 1997.

Brandão, José Antonio. *"Your fyre shall burn no more": Iroquois Policy toward New France and Its Native Allies to 1701*. University of Nebraska Press, Lincoln and London, 1997.

Brandão, José Antonio and William A. Starna. "The Treaties of 1701: A Triumph of Iroquois Diplomacy," *Ethnohistory*, Vol. 43 (Spring 1996), pp. 209-244.

Brown, Craig, ed. *The Illustrated History of Canada*. Lester & Orpen Dennys, Toronto, 1987.

Champagne, André, ed. *L'histoire du Régime français*. Septentrion/Radio Canada, Quebec/Montreal, 1996.

Delâge, Denys. *Bitter Feast: Amerindians and Europeans in the American Northeast, 1600-64*. Jane Brierley, transl. University of British Columbia Press, Vancouver, 1993.

Delâge, Denys. "L'alliance franco-amérindienne, 1660-1701," *Recherches amérindiennes au Québec*, Montreal, Vol. 19, No. 1 (1989), pp. 3-15.

Delâge, Denys. "Les Iroquois chrétiens des réductions, 1667-1770, I: migration et rapports avec les Français," *Recherches amérindiennes au Québec*, Montreal, Vol. 21, No. 1-2 (1991), pp. 59-70.

Delâge, Denys. "Les Iroquois chrétiens des réductions, 1667-1770, II: rapports avec la Ligue iroquoise, les Britanniques et les autres nations autochtones," *Recherches amérindiennes au Québec*, Montreal, Vol. 21, No. 3 (1991), pp. 39-50.

Delâge, Denys. "L'influence des Amérindiens sur les Canadiens et les Français au temps de la Nouvelle-France," *Lekton*, 2 (2) (1992), pp. 103-191.

Desrosiers, Léo-Paul. *Iroquoisie*. Septentrion, Quebec, 1998, 4 vol.

Dickason, Olive P. *Canada's First Nations: A History of Founding Peoples from Earliest Times*. McClelland and Stewart, Toronto, 1992.

Dupuis, Renée. *La question indienne au Canada*. Boréal, Montreal, 1991.
Eccles, William J. *Canada under Louis XIV, 1663–1701*. McClelland and Stewart, Toronto, 1964.

Eid, Leroy. "The Ojibwa-Iroquois War: The War the Five Nations Did Not Win," *Ethnohistory*, Vol. 26 (Fall 1979), pp. 297-324.

Grabowski, Jan. "Les Amérindiens domiciliés et la 'contrebande' des fourrures en Nouvelle-France," *Recherches amérindiennes au Québec*, Montreal, Vol. 24, No. 3 (1994), pp. 45-52.

Havard, Gilles. "Paix et interculturalité en Nouvelle-France au temps de Louis XIV," *Recherches amérindiennes au Québec*, Montreal, Vol. 27, No. 2 (1997), pp. 3-18.

Havard, Gilles. *The Great Peace of Montreal of 1701: French–Native Diplomacy in the Seventeenth Century*. Phyllis Aronoff and Howard Scott, transl. McGill-Queen's University Press, Montreal, 2001.

Havard, Gilles, ed. *Le temps des alliances: la Grande Paix de Montréal de 1701*. Recherches amérindiennes au Québec, vol. 31, no. 2 (2001).

Jaenen, Cornelius J. *Friend and Foe: Aspects of French–Amerindian Cultural Contact in the Sixteenth and Seventeenth Centuries*. McClelland and Stewart, Toronto, 1976.

Jennings , Francis. *The Invasion of America: Indians, Colonialism, and the Cant of Conquest*. W.W. Norton Library, New York, 1976.

Jennings, Francis. *The Ambiguous Iroquois Empire: The Covenant Chain Confederation of Indian Tribes with English Colonies, from its Beginnings to the Lancaster Treaty of 1744*. W.W. Norton, New York, 1984.

Jennings, Francis, ed. *The History and Culture of Iroquois Diplomacy: An Interdisciplinary Guide to the Treaties of the Six Nations and Their League*. Syracuse University Press, Syracuse, 1985.

Jetten, Marc. *Enclaves amérindiennes: les "réductions" du Canada 1637-1701*. Septentrion, Quebec, 1994.

Mathieu, Jacques. *La Nouvelle-France: les Français en Amérique du Nord, XVIe - XVIIIe siècle*. Presses de l'Université Laval, Belin [France] and Quebec, 1991.

Miquelon, Dale. *New France, 1701-1744: "A Supplement to Europe"*. McClelland and Stewart, Toronto, 1987.

Richter, Daniel K. *The Ordeal of the Longhouse: The Peoples of the Iroquois League in the Era of European Colonization*. University of North Carolina Press, Chapel Hill, 1992.

Savard, Rémi. *L'Algonquin Tessouat et la fondation de Montréal: diplomatie franco-indienne en Nouvelle-France*. L'Hexagone, Montreal, 1996.

Sawaya, Jean Pierre. *La fédération des Sept feux de la vallée du Saint-Laurent, XVIIe-XIXe siècle*. Septentrion, Quebec, 1998.

Trigger, Bruce Graham. *The Children of Aataentsic: A History of the Huron People to 1660*. McGill-Queen's University Press, Montreal, 2 vol., 1976.

Trigger, Bruce Graham. *Natives and Newcomers: Canada's "Heroic Age" Reconsidered*. McGill-Queen's University Press, Montreal, 1985.

Vaugeois, Denis, ed. *Les Hurons de Lorette*. Septentrion, Quebec, 1996.

Viau, Roland. *Enfants du néant et mangeurs d'âme: guerre, culture et société en Iroquoisie ancienne*. Boréal, Montreal, 1997.

Viau, Roland. *Femmes de personne: sexes, genres et pouvoirs en Iroquoisie ancienne*. Boréal, Montréal, 2000.

White, Richard. *The Middle Ground: Indians, Empires and Republics in the Great Lakes Region, 1650-1815*. Cambridge University Press, New York, 1991.

Zoltvany, Yves F. *Philippe de Rigaud de Vaudreuil: Governor of New France, 1703-1725*. McClelland and Stewart, Toronto, 1974.